Black Heritage Bible Lessons Volume 2

"Teaching the History of the African Race Directly from the Bible"

# BLACK CITIZENS OF ZION

BY

STEPHEN L. WILLIAMS SR.

"*A Study of five Black Empires of the Bible*"

PUBLISHED BY SDAHOSTING
*WWW.SDAHOSTING.COM*
BRIDGEPORT CT 06606

BLACK CITIZENS OF ZION

© Copyright 1993 by Stephen L. Williams Sr.

All scripture passages are quoted from the *The King James Version*, (Cambridge: Cambridge) 1769 unless otherewise stated.

Cover designed by Wanderlie Di Silva

ISBN NUMBER 1-59196-015-9

All Rights Reserved. No part of this book shall be reproduced, stored in a retrieval system, or transmitted by any means without written permission from the author.

## TABLE OF CONTENTS

**CONDITION OF BLACK AMERICA** — 7

*GOD'S FEELINGS TOWARD ZION.* — 11

**ZION** — 12
**MELCHIZEDEK** — 15

*THE GLORIES OF ZION* — 21

**SABBATH** — 23
**THE PAPACY** — 25

**EGYPTIAN CITIZENS OF ZION** — 37

**MENES** — 40
**ISRAEL** — 42
**MIDIANITES** — 43
**THE EXODUS** — 46
**JOSHUA** — 46
**EGYPTIAN TEACHINGS** — 49

**BABYLONIAN CITIZENS OF ZION** — 51

**TYRIAN OR PHOENICIAN CITIZENS OF ZION** — 65

**PHILISTINE CITIZENS OF ZION** — 79

**ETHIOPIAN CITIZENS OF ZION** — 89

| | |
|---|---|
| **MOHAMMED CE 570-632** | 99 |
| **BLACK MUSLIMS – NATION OF ISLAM** | 103 |
| **JESUS CHRIST BCE 4 - CE 27** | 105 |
| **PROOF OF JESUS' LORDSHIP.** | 107 |
| **HIS BIRTH** | 108 |
| **BETRAYED BY FRIENDS** | 109 |
| **PRICE OF BETRAYAL** | 109 |
| **NO BROKEN BONES:** | 110 |
| **RESURRECTION:** | 110 |

# DEDICATION

This book is dedicated to my parents for investing their finances in my future. To my mother-in law who gave me my first set of Bible Commentary which started me on this quest for knowledge. To the many who encouraged me on my way especially the Solid Rock Seventh Day Adventist Church members who challenged me to greater heights in scholarship. Most of all to my wife Cellierose who endured my busyness and to my children Stephen and Natalie who have been praying for the end of this book so they can enjoy the proceeds. Then finally to my twins Jennifer and Jonathan: Jennifer whose cuddles always forces me to take a break from whatever I am doing and Jonathan, because his diligence and willingness to help in everything is a constant source of encouragement to a busy father.

Black Citizens of Zion

# INTRODUCTION

## CONDITION OF BLACK AMERICA

It is with some apprehension that Blacks look over the path our ancestors have traveled, especially in North America. To use the words of the Black National Anthem,

> *"We have come, over a way that with tears has been watered,*
> *We have come, treading our path through the blood of the slaughtered,*
> *Out from the gloomy past, till now we stand at last,*
> *Where the white gleam of our bright star is cast."*

The road on which the ancestors of present day African-Americans traveled was fraught with peril and danger on every hand. Men and women died trying to bring Blacks freedom from slavery, miss-education and bigotry. It is true that Blacks have made tremendous progress, but all must confess this community still has a long way to go.

Today many African-American walk the streets unable to find jobs-to use the terminology of today, they are unprepared, unqualified, or over qualified. Young men of color many times find it easier to sell drugs than stay in school, while the community that can least afford it, is overran with drug distribution and sale. To further complicate this, in many poor neighborhoods, the children can point out to many new comers in his community homes where drugs are readily available, while law enforcers seems bewildered as to where these crack houses are and what to do about them.

African-American males are jailed more often than any other segment of our community. This robs their sons of the role model they need to grow up to be what God would have them to be, and steals from the Black female the spouses they need who are capable of providing for them a rich and fulfilling live.

It has been said, that black women finds it easier to get a job than a Black male does. If this is true, she is being forced to be the breadwinner of the home, and this robs him of the self esteem he needs to properly accomplish his rightful role. Then add to this the problem of baby sitters training our children, and we begin to see why the Black family is quickly loosing its wholeness and its ability to train strong leaders for tomorrow.

Furthermore many inner City School districts have now decided that inner city kids must be taught sexual education by unchristian teachers. This I believe has led to an increase in immorality and venereal diseases among our youth. Some school districts now give our children condoms free of charge without parental consent, as if to say, sleep with whomever you want, whenever you want, just protect yourselves. Abortion has become proper birth control and AIDS is rampant in our community. It is as if the Black community is being placed on a path that will lead to the production of genetically inferior children.

As we evaluate this information, the question, can the Black race survive? Becomes a legitimate question, because the sad reality is that even in the churches, which are believed to be the strongest sector of the Black community, children are born out of wedlock in record numbers. We are facing a situation where numerous single Black women have three and four children, and struggle alone in an attempt to meet the educational and emotional needs of these children.

These indeed are troublesome times for Black Americans. Yet despite the ravages of our time and the consistent attempt to destroy Black families and their morality, despite the miss-education, under-education and foolishness Blacks encounter, they do not live in a hopeless condition, because God has promised never to leave them alone.

# CONDITION OF BLACK AMERICA

Islam would have us believe that the Bible is the white man's book. It would have us accept the Muslim as our brothers in adversity, opposing the injustice of a capitalistic society.

History, however, does not support this position. According to history, it was Islam that first moved into Africa and destroyed the motherland and sold the African-American's ancestors into slavery. It was the Arabic converts to Islam who first began a world wide trade of Black slaves. The coming of Capitalistic Europe only replaced the Muslims who first enslaved the African people.

The reality is, and always will be, that the best way for African-Americans to ensure a healthy survival is to accept Jesus as Lord and Savior. A Jesus whom it can be demonstrated was of African descent, chose Black disciples, and spent much of His ministry ministering to Black people.

Very few are aware that the Bible, is concerned about all races. Most believe it is concerned only with the Jews and very few are aware that much of the Bible was written by Africans and speaks extensively about Africans.

The purpose of this book is to reveal the origin and racial make of the various nations mentioned in the 87th Psalm. It will help all to see that when the names of the redeemed are checked from the "Book of Life," when God's children are mentioned, standing around the great throne of God Almighty, Black people drawn from the nations of Philistia, Babylonia, Egypt, Ethiopia along with Phoenicia will be there, all of them, "Black Citizens of Zion!!"

Black Citizens of Zion

[11] Let mount Zion rejoice, let the daughters of Judah be glad, because of thy judgments. [12] Walk about Zion, and go round about her: tell the towers thereof. [13] Mark ye well her bulwarks, consider her palaces; that ye may tell *it* to the generation following. Psalm 48:11-13.

# "AFRICA" – HOME OF THE BLACKS

# CHAPTER 1

## *GOD'S FEELINGS TOWARD ZION.*

*"His foundation is in the holy mountains. 2 The LORD loveth the gates of Zion more than all the dwellings of Jacob. 3 Glorious things are spoken of thee, O city of God. Selah. 4 I will make mention of Rahab and Babylon to them that know me: behold Philistia, and Tyre, with Ethiopia; this man was born there. 5 And of Zion it shall be said, This and that man was born in her: and the highest himself shall establish her. 6 The LORD shall count, when he writeth up the people, that this man was born there. Selah. 7 As well the singers as the players on instruments shall be there: all my springs are in thee." (Psalm 87)*

The above Psalm was penned by the Sons of Korah. Their father Korah along with Datham and Abiram had challenged the authority of Moses as they traveled to the Promised Land. According to the Bible, the earth opened and swallowed them and their families, except for some of the children of Korah.

Now, as priests of the temple of God, they played their rightful role. They are careful in what they do and say. They do not challenge the authority of God's elected servant, but are respectful of leadership, since they have learnt firsthand the results of rebellion.

The proclamation of the word is now their number one priority along with the ministry of music. In this Psalm we see them reflecting upon God's goodness and marveling at God's ability to save to the utmost. In this state of marvel and utter excitement they declared:

> *"The LORD loveth the gates of Zion more than all the dwellings of Jacob." (Psalm 87:2)*

It is imperative for African-Americans to understand Zion, its origin and its final establishment. This is necessary because Zion was originally black men's territory, specifically belonging to the sons of Ham. Let us therefore take a historical look at Zion and God's feelings toward Zion.

## ZION

The first thing that needs to be noted is that Zion and Jerusalem refer to the same city. In the time of Abraham this city was known as Salem. Salem was the city of a Hametic King Priest called Melchizedek. The reader will discover later in this book the evidence that Ham was the father of the Black race, and his descendants were black, Melchizedek being one of these descendants.

Melchizedek was representative of Jesus Christ on earth before the Hebrew Levitical System was organized. This we can assume for the following reasons: 1. He is called a Priest of the most High God, before the Priesthood is organized. (Hebrews 7:1) 2. Jesus is made a Priest like unto him, in the New Testament, and not unto Levite. (Hebrews 5:10) These facts will be discussed later.

Zion was first called Jerusalem by the Canaanites. The Canaanites were decedents of Canaan. Canaan was the Black son of Ham.[1] It was Canaan's descendants along with those of

---

[1] We say he was the Black son of Ham because Ham is the strongest word in the Egyptian tongue for blackness, and is generally accepted to be the father of the Black race. If in fact Ham was the father of the black race and black himself, then according to the standards of genetics, he could only produce a Black child.

## GOD'S FEELINGS TOWARD ZION.

his brothers that dominated Palestine, Syria and Africa. Later, during the time of Samson and the Judges, Zion was known as Jebus, home of the black race called the Jebusites.[2] It was from the Jebusites that David king of Israel later took the city. The Prophet Samuel writes:

> *"6 And the king and his men went to Jerusalem unto the Jebusites, the inhabitants of the land: which spake unto David, saying, Except thou take away the blind and the lame, thou shalt not come in hither: thinking, David cannot come in hither. 7 Nevertheless David took the stronghold of Zion: the same is the city of David." (2 Samuel 2:6 & 7)*

The Jebusites remained in the city after the conquest of David. They intermarried with the Children of Israel and were quite at home with the Kings of African descent that sat on the throne of David.[3] This Black lineage began with Saul who was of the tribe of Benjamin, and continued with David himself.[4] In fact according to the following verses, the taking of Black Canaanite wives was very popular among "The Chosen People of God."

---

[2] The Jebusites according to Genesis 10 were descendants of Ham, Father of the Black race.

[3] When the Children of Israel migrated to the continent of Africa, there were only 77 of them, many of whom were already Hamites. Two hundred and fifty years later, there were millions. No nation could grow from 77 to millions in two hundred years. Most of the people, who therefore left Egypt, must have been Africans themselves. These were the children of Israel. For a deeper study, see the book, "Black Man in the Old Testament". Furthermore David is a descendant of Rahab the African and Ruth the Moabite.

[4] The Bible informs us that the tribe of Benjamin at one time was allowed to marry only Black women because of their sin of rape executed against a traveling Levite and his concubine. If this is true, then in just a few generations, even if the Benjamites were not originally Africans, which they probably were, they would soon be considered Africans.

## Black Citizens of Zion

> *"Ezra 9:2 For they have taken of their daughters for themselves, and for their sons: so that the holy seed have mingled themselves with the people of those lands."*
> *"Judges 3:5 5 And the children of Israel dwelt among the Canaanites, Hittites, and Amorites, and Perizzites, and Hivites, and Jebusites: 6 And they took their daughters to be their wives, and gave their daughters to their sons, and served their God's."*

Zion was the resting place for the Ark of the Covenant, and its name was immortalized when the name was applied to the city of the Redeemed.

God was jealous for this predominantly Black city. He desired that Children dance in the streets and that people of all races be represented there. He loved Zion more than all other cities, not because God was partial, but because God had ordained that from Zion, all men would come to know Him.

Zion was to send missionaries to the world at large, pointing men to the true way of Yahweh, God of the universe. Zion was to be the capital of the world, it was ordained to be the city of all men and all races.

The prophets wrote the following concerning Zion.

> *"Psalms 76:2 In Salem also is his tabernacle, and his dwelling place in Zion."*
> *"Psalms 48:2 Beautiful for situation, the joy of the whole earth, is mount Zion.".*
> *"Jeremiah 3:17 At that time they shall call Jerusalem the throne of the LORD; and all the nations shall be gathered unto it, to the name of the LORD, to Jerusalem: neither shall they walk any more after the imagination of their evil heart."(KJV)*
> *"2 King 19:34 For I will defend this city, to save it, for mine own sake,"*

GOD'S FEELINGS TOWARD ZION.

Thus we see from the above quotations, that Zion is special to God, not because David had established it, but Zion is God's city. It was God's city during the time of Abraham when Melchizedek, the great Black Priest King ruled there.

## MELCHIZEDEK

According to the Bible, Melchizedek was a monarch who had no beginning or end, no mother or father. This king was a representative of God on earth. It was to Melchizedek that Abraham, Father of the Jews brought his tithe and his offering. Melchizedek was regarded as an anti-typical Jesus, and some scholars suggest that Melchizedek was Christ Himself.

The Jews look with glee upon the Priesthood of Aaron. It is with fond memories that they reflect upon the one through whom along with his descendants God had ordained a system for salvation. This system was imperfect but powerful, whereby the sinner, who strayed from God, could find himself in right relationship with God. It was a system that became revered the world over, and the whole nation was organized around this Levitical system.

The system demanded that the sick or diseased before they could be declared clean, must present themselves to the priest. The king if he would be chosen must be anointed by the priest. The nation dared not go to war, unless directed by God through the priest. This Levitical Priesthood was indeed powerful, yet with all its power, it could not compare to the Priesthood of the black king Melchizedek.

Melchizedek was an Amorite king. (Genesis 10) It was he who ruled over the city of Salem. Salem of course, later became known as Jerusalem, city of David. It appears that long before Salem became the city of Jerusalem, it was the city of God. It may have been the city of God for thousands of years before we first encounter it, because even though we have no record of God choosing Jerusalem before the coming of the Israelites, when the father of the Israelite's was introduced to us in the

Black Citizens of Zion

book of Genesis, he is presented as bowing before Melchizedek king of Salem, and presenting to him his tithe.

This suggests that Melchizedek was far more powerful than Abraham. Yet, the real power of the Priesthood of Melchizedek is not best represented in Abraham bowing before him. The real power is demonstrated in the fact that God ordains Jesus a Priest not after the order of the Jewish Priesthood, but after the Hametic Priesthood of Melchizedek. These Black Amorites were worshipers of the true God, because Melchizedek their king and Priest was "Priest of the most High God," Yahweh himself. Read what the Apostle Paul states in his letter to the Hebrews:

> *"Hebrews 7:1 For this Melchisedec, king of Salem, priest of the most high God, who met Abraham returning from the slaughter of the kings, and blessed him; 2 To whom also Abraham gave a tenth part of all; first being by interpretation king of righteousness, and after that also king of Salem, which is, king of peace; 3 Without father, without mother, without descent, having neither beginning of days, nor end of life; but made like unto the Son of God; abideth a priest continually. 7:4 Now consider how great this man was, unto whom even the patriarch Abraham gave the tenth of the spoils."*

Christ when he was on earth, made clear His feelings for Zion. He was fully aware that the people of Zion would put Him to death, yet that did not change His feelings towards this city.

Listen to the words of Jesus:

> *"MAT 23:37 O Jerusalem, Jerusalem, thou that killest the prophets, and stonest them which are sent unto thee, how often would I have gathered thy children together, even as a hen gathereth her chickens under her wings, and ye would not"*

## GOD'S FEELINGS TOWARD ZION.

During those times when God was forced to bring judgment upon Zion because its citizens refused to be the example God required, God's feelings never changed towards this predominantly Black city.

The Prophet Zechariah wrote:

> *Zechariah 8:1 "Again the word of the LORD of hosts came to me, saying, 2 Thus saith the LORD of hosts; I was jealous for Zion with great jealousy, and I was jealous for her with great fury."*

Furthermore, God's plan was to return to Zion when His people came to their senses. Consider the following passage:

> *Zechariah 8:3 "Thus saith the LORD; I am returned unto Zion, and will dwell in the midst of Jerusalem: and Jerusalem shall be called a city of truth; and the mountain of the LORD of hosts the holy mountain."*

Zion itself was originally given to the tribe of Benjamin when the land was divided among the twelve tribes[5]. It later passed to the tribe of Judah that began as a tribe of Black descent through Judah and his Canaanite daughter in law. This heritage continued through the numerous Canaanites and Egyptians who married into the tribe and became the lineage through whom King David and then Christ the Messiah eventually came.

It is important to note that all of Palestine at the time of the Israelite conquest was Hametic and thus of black descent. It stands to reason therefore, that wherever the Children of Israel settled and did not drive out the inhabitants, as is indicated in the following passage, the people and Israel became one.

---

[5] "Judges 1:21 And the children of Benjamin did not drive out the Jebusites that inhabited Jerusalem; but the Jebusites dwell with the children of Benjamin in Jerusalem unto this day."

## Black Citizens of Zion

> *Judges 1:21 "And the children of Benjamin did not drive out the Jebusites that inhabited Jerusalem; but the Jebusites dwell with the children of Benjamin in Jerusalem unto this day."*

Thus Benjamin co-habited with the Black race that dwelled in Salem. This is fascinating when one considers that according to the ridiculous prophecy of Noah, which is commonly taught by popular religious scholars today, the Canaanites, unlike the other sons of Ham, were cursed. Yet these cursed sons of Ham were the ones who ultimately became ancestors of Jesus Christ because of their intermarriage with the Jewish people.

If one is to take the book of Judges seriously, it may very well mean that by the time Christ was born, the Jews might have lost totally their Shemite features, and looked more like the Canaanites, and were considered Ethiopians as Homer and Herodotus were to write. Consider the following passages from Judges 1 and 3.

> *"27 Neither did Manasseh drive out the inhabitants of Bethshean and her towns, nor Taanach and her towns, nor the inhabitants of Dor and her towns, nor the inhabitants of Ibleam and her towns, nor the inhabitants of Megiddo and her towns: but the Canaanites would dwell in that land. 28 And it came to pass, when Israel was strong, that they put the Canaanites to tribute, and did not utterly drive them out.*
>
> *29 Neither did Ephraim drive out the Canaanites that dwelt in Gezer; but the Canaanites dwelt in Gezer among them. 30 Neither did Zebulun drive out the inhabitants of Kitron, nor the inhabitants of Nahalol; but the Canaanites dwelt among them, and became tributaries.*
>
> *31 Neither did Asher drive out the inhabitants of Accho, nor the inhabitants of Zidon, nor of Ahlab, nor of Achzib, nor of Helbah, nor of Aphik, nor of Rehob: 32 But the Asherites dwelt among the Canaanites, the inhabitants of the land: for they did not drive them out.*

# GOD'S FEELINGS TOWARD ZION.

> *33 Neither did Naphtali drive out the inhabitants of Beth-she'mesh, nor the inhabitants of Bethanath; but he dwelt among the Canaanites, the inhabitants of the land: nevertheless the inhabitants of Beth-she'mesh and of Bethanath became tributaries unto them. "*
>
> *"Judges 3:1 1 Now these are the nations which the LORD left, to prove Israel by them, 3 Namely, five lords of the Philistines, and all the Canaanites, and the Sidonians, and the Hivites that dwelt in mount Lebanon, from mount Baalhermon unto the entering in of Hamath."*

As we turn our attention to the glories of Zion, all people of African descent must take pride that these glories belong not only to the Jews as is commonly presented by modern scholars, but also to the Sons of Ham. These sons of Ham who were the original inhabitants of Zion, continued to live in Zion and became assimilated into the Jewish race, or dare I say, the Jewish race became assimilated into the Canaanite race? Let us now turn our attention to some of the glories of historic and future Zion.

Black Citizens of Zion

**Sphinx of Tarhaka Pharaoh of Egypt 690-664 BCE**

In times past, when war was coming, it was to Africa that men looked for military assistance. It was the men of Africa that had the might and ability to defeat the coming armies. When Senecharib was at the gates of Jerusalem and commanded Hezekiah to surrender the city, it was to Africa that word was sent, "come quickly, deliver your brothers from the hand of the king of Assyria", and Shitbitku ruler of Nubia, sent his brother Tarhaka to the assistance of the Black king Hezekiah, ruler of Israel.

# CHAPTER 2

## *THE GLORIES OF ZION*

*"Glorious things are spoken of thee, O city of God"*
*(Psalm 87:3)*

One of the problems many have with understanding the Bible is embedded in the fact that the Bible speaks in historical, future and present realities. Then there are Conditional prophecies which has future significance base on our present actions. The city of Zion is historical as well as prophetic. One is thus forced to decide to which reality the various references belong.

The Bible presents Zion as being a very glorious city. This refers to the Zion of the past, as well as the future. God Himself will be the architect of future Zion, and judging by the job God has done in making both humanity and the Universe, the future city of Zion promises to be something extraordinary.

> *HEBREWS 11:16 "But now they desire a better country, that is, an heavenly: wherefore God is not ashamed to be called their God: for he hath prepared for them a city."*

Note the facts the Bible reveals about the city God has promised to prepare:

1. The city will descend from heaven as a bride. (Revelation 21:1) 2. It stands 216 feet high, and 315 miles on each side, with Jasper walls. 3. It has twelve gates made from solid pearls and streets laid with pure gold. 4. Its twelve foundations

## Black Citizens of Zion

are poured from many different precious metals such as Jasper, sapphire, emerald and topaz to name a few. 5. This city has an amazing tree called the tree of life. 6. Whenever one eats from this tree, it brings life and keeps away sickness. 7. Zion will eventually come from heaven to earth, and no sinners or wicked person will live there. John the Revelator writes.

>*Revelation 21 "3 And I John saw the holy city, new Jerusalem, coming down from God out of heaven, prepared as a bride adorned for her husband...*
>
>*21:4 And God shall wipe away all tears from their eyes; and there shall be no more death, neither sorrow, nor crying, neither shall there be any more pain: for the former things are passed away...*
>
>*21:11 Having the glory of God: and her light was like unto a stone most precious, even like a jasper stone, clear as crystal; 21:12 And had a wall great and high, and had twelve gates, and at the gates twelve angels, and names written thereon, which are the names of the twelve tribes of the children of Israel...*
>
>*21:14 And the wall of the city had twelve foundations, and in them the names of the twelve apostles of the Lamb...*
>
>*21:16 And the city lieth foursquare, and the length is as large as the breadth: and he measured the city with the reed, twelve thousand furlongs. The length and the breadth and the height of it are equal...*
>
>*21:18 And the building of the wall of it was of jasper: and the city was pure gold, like unto clear glass. 21:19 And the foundations of the wall of the city were garnished with all manner of precious stones. The first foundation was jasper; the second, sapphire; the third, a chalcedony; the fourth, an emerald; 21:20 The fifth, sardonyx; the sixth, sardius; the seventh, chrysolite; the eighth, beryl; the ninth, a topaz; the tenth, a chrysoprasus; the eleventh, a jacinth; the twelfth, an amethyst. 21:21 And the twelve gates were twelve pearls;*

# THE GLORIES OF ZION

*every several gate was of one pearl: and the street of the city was pure gold, as it were transparent glass. 21:22 And I saw no temple therein: for the Lord God Almighty and the Lamb are the temple of it. 21:23 And the city had no need of the sun, neither of the moon, to shine in it: for the glory of God did lighten it, and the Lamb is the light thereof."*

The Bible also declares that Jesus will reside in the city, and other citizens will build houses and plant the gardens of their dreams there. There will be no death, sickness, jealousy, hatred, bigotry or prejudice, the sea will be like glass, animals will be tame and there will be no deserts.

## THE SABBATH

In Zion, men will worship before Yahweh and sing his praises on His day. Every Sabbath will be a time of refreshing worship. People will take the time to visit with their Creator and thank Him for His goodness in allowing them to be citizens of Zion. The prophet Isaiah writes concerning the Sabbath.

*Isaiah 66:22 "For as the new heavens and the new earth, which I will make, shall remain before me, saith the LORD, so shall your seed and your name remain. 66:23 And it shall come to pass, that from one new moon to another, and from one Sabbath to another, shall all flesh come to worship before me, saith the LORD."*

The Sabbath was given to Adam in the Garden of Eden on the continent of Africa. When it was first instituted by God, it was established on Saturday the Seventh Day of the week. It was here in the home of the first man, that God blessed, hollowed and sanctified the Sabbath.

*"Thus the heavens and the earth were finished, and all the host of them. ²And on the seventh day God ended his work which he had made; and he rested on the seventh*

## Black Citizens of Zion

*day from all his work which he had made. ³And God blessed the seventh day, and sanctified it: because that in it he had rested from all his work which God created and made." (Genesis 2:1-3)*

Africans therefore, which included Adam, were the first keepers of the Sabbath. It was from Africa that Sabbath worship spread to Palestine and then the world. The Sabbath is not Jewish as some miss-informed priests and pseudo-scholars would have us believe. The Jews accepted the Sabbath when it was restated on the Mount and written on the tables of stone after their release from slavery. The Sabbath existed long before there was ever a Jew. It existed from the creation of the earth. Moses, who wrote the book of Genesis while he was living with the Black Midianites, wrote:[6]

*Genesis 2:2 "And on the seventh day God ended his work which he had made; and he rested on the seventh day from all his work which he had made. 2:3 And God blessed the seventh day, and sanctified it: because that in it he had rested from all his work which God created and made."*

The Sabbath is eternal. It existed before sin, and it will exist after sin. It is a perpetual sign that God is man's creator. This was the general belief which prevailed until the Nation of Rome defeated the city states of Carthage and became a world power.

Sabbath keeping began to change when the Sons of Japheth (Caucasians or Whites, commonly called Europeans) began to inherit the tents of Shem (Jews). When the Romans accepted Christianity, they instituted what was later to be called the Papacy and took upon them the prerogative to change time and God's law.

---

[6] The Midianites were the descendants of an African woman named Keturah and Abraham the father of the Jews. They were faithful in the keeping of God's law when the children of Israel were lost in slavery.

# THE GLORIES OF ZION

## THE PAPACY

*"The Pope is of so great dignity and so exalted that he is not a mere man, but as it were God, and the vicar of God....He is likewise the divine monarch and supreme emperor and king of kings so that if it be possible that the angels err the faith, they could be judged and excommunicated by the pope." (The Roman Catholic Eccleastical dictionary)*

*"The church has changed Sabbath...from Sabbath to Sunday not by the command of Christ but by its own authority" (Holtzman, Canon and Traditions P. 263)*

The above quotes attest to the arrogance of Roman Catholicism. The boast of their power emphasized in the change of the Sabbath. This change, according to the Bible, the Papacy would attempt, and it would lead to the wearing out of the saints of the Most High God.

Read what Daniel has to say concerning Papal Rome in the Daniel 7:23-25.

*"23 Thus he said, The fourth beast shall be the fourth kingdom upon earth, which shall be diverse from all kingdoms, and shall devour the whole earth, and shall tread it down, and break it in pieces. 24 And the ten horns out of this kingdom are ten kings that shall arise: and another shall rise after them; and he shall be diverse from the first, and he shall subdue three kings. 25 And he shall speak great words against the most High, and shall wear out the saints of the most High, and think to change times and laws: and they shall be given into his hand until a time and times and the dividing of time."*

The Papacy tried to force this change upon all Christians and was successful everywhere except on the continent of Africa. Here the Ethiopians for generations continued the biblical teaching of Sabbath keeping when the Catholic Church forced all others to follow her in this apostasy. Ellen G. Whites states.

> *"The History of the church in Ethiopia and Abyssinia is especially significant. Amid the Gloom of the dark ages, The Christians of Central Africa were lost sight of and forgotten by the world, and for many centuries they enjoyed freedom and the exercise of their faith, but at last Rome learnt of their existence and the Emperor of Abyssinia was soon beguiled into an acknowledgment of the pope as the Vicar of Christ. Other concessions followed. An edict was issued forbidding the observance of the Sabbath under the severest penalty."* [7]

Capitalism soon completed the work Rome had begun. The desire for money and riches has led many to disregard God's law of rest and spiritual growth. Love of riches has replaced mans dedication to God. Every person of African descent must become aware however that Sunday keeping is a European institution. It is simply another attempt by colonial powers to enslave the Africans. Blacks should endeavor to return to God's 7th Day Sabbath. They have always been people of the Bible, and nowhere in scripture is there recommendation for a change from Sabbath to Sunday by Jesus or His disciples.

There are a number of reasons that contributed to the change of the Sabbath from the Seventh Day to the First Day which are worth exploring.

After the death of Jesus, and the fall of the Holy Spirit some 50 days later, there was a tremendous growth in the Church. People of all races, color and creed began to accept Jesus as Savior and turn to Him in large numbers.

Quickly the Africans who had been traveling to Jerusalem for centuries spread the word in their homeland that the Messiah

---

[7] White, E. G. *Spirit if Prophecy Vol. 1*. (Mountain View California: Pacific Press Publishing Association), 578.

# THE GLORIES OF ZION

had come. The Ethiopian Eunuch sent by Candice Amanateree had no doubt convinced the Ethiopian people that the Messiah of David had finally come and died for the sins of the people. The Eunuch obviously believed this because the Bible says he was baptized by Philip. The devil then got angry. He had tried all he could to put an end to Jesus and His followers, but it was not working.

>"*Paganism realized that should the gospel triumph, her temples and altars would be swept away, therefore she summoned her forces to destroy Christianity. The fires of persecution were kindled. Christians were stripped of their possessions and driven from their homes. They were crucified and burnt, sealing their testimony with their blood. Nobles, slaves, rich, poor, learned and ignorant alike were slain without mercy.*
>
>*Christians were accused of the most dreadful crimes. They were held responsible for the greatest calamities. Famine, pestilence and earth-quake were blamed upon them. They were condemned as rebels against the empire, as foes of religion and pest to society. Great numbers were thrown to wild beasts or burned alive in the amphitheaters. Some were crucified; some were covered with the skins of wild animals and thrust into the arena to be torn by dogs. Multitudes watched and jeered as their dying agonies went up to God in a plea for help.*
>
>*Under the fiercest persecution these witnesses for Jesus kept their faith. Though deprived of every comfort they uttered no complaint. In vain were Satan's efforts to destroy the church of Christ by violence. The gospel continued to spread and multitude continued to call on*

## Black Citizens of Zion

*the name of Jesus. Thousands died horrible death, and thousands more simply converted to fill their positions."*[8]

Satan then devised a new plan. What he could not accomplish through persecution, he would accomplish through trickery. He would plant his banner in the Christian Church. He would align Paganism and Christianity, and call it by a new name, Catholicism.

Thus persecution ended, and prosperity began. Idolaters were led to receive a part of the Christian faith while they rejected others. The barbarians knocking at the gates of Rome were allowed to profess to accept Jesus as the Son of God, but felt no need of repentance or of a change of heart.

The church was in peril. What prison, torture, fire and sword were not able to do, prosperity achieved. A union between Christianity and Paganism took place. The objects of pagan worship were exchanged for Christian objects. The Black Madonna was replaced with her European counterpart. Sunday the day of the Sun, took the place of the Seventh Day Sabbath ordained by God, and the African Church and the Roman church went their separate way. The Romans followed paganism, while the African church was lost sight of. Christianity entered a new era.

Satan had offered Jesus the world, if only He bowed down and worship Him, now he does the same thing with men. Jesus had responded, "Thou shall worship the Lord thy God, and Him only shall thou serve". (Luke 4:8.)

Men however responded differently. We accepted the gifts of Satan. The church then became powerful on earth, but weakened in God's sight. The papacy was invested with authority over all Bishops and Pastors. He was soon regarded as infallible, which means he is God and demands the homage of all men. This lead to the banning of the Bible which could

---

[8] White, E. G. *Spirit if Prophecy Vol. 1*. (Mountain View California: Pacific Press Publishing Association), 579.

## THE GLORIES OF ZION

not be used to support the positions the Church was now taking. People were not allowed to have Bibles in their homes and the priest and Papacy came to be accepted as the universal representative of God on earth.

The Sabbath Day became a day of fasting, and Sunday a day of celebration. The Dark Ages had begun. Then as the power of the church increased, the dark ages deepened. Faith was transferred from Christ to the papacy. Men were taught the papacy was the mediator, and no one could come to Christ without coming to Him. Long pilgrimage, acts of penance, the worships of relics, the erection of churches, shrines and altars, the payments of large sum of money to the church were done to appease the wrath of God. Everyone had forgotten that God had commanded:

> *Exodus 20:4 "Thou shalt not make unto thee any graven image, or any likeness of any thing that is in heaven above, or that is in the earth beneath, or that is in the water under the earth: Exodus 20:5 Thou shalt not bow down thyself to them, nor serve them: for I the LORD thy God am a jealous God, visiting the iniquity of the fathers upon the children unto the third and fourth generation of them that hate me; Exodus 20:6 And showing mercy unto thousands of them that love me, and keep my commandments."*

Image worships became acceptable. Candles were burnt before images in the custom of the pagans. The mass replaced the communion; purgatory was created to put fear in men's heart and penance to remove that fear.

The worst of Rome's inventions was the inquisition. Because of this dreaded institution, the mangled form of Millions cried out to God for vengeance upon this apostate power. From Europe to the new world, millions were massacred in the name of religion.

Black Citizens of Zion

God had described the Empire of Rome in the following way to the prophet Daniel:

> *Dan 7:7 After this I saw in the night visions, and behold a fourth beast, dreadful and terrible, and strong exceedingly; and it had great iron teeth: it devoured and brake in pieces, and stamped the residue with the feet of it: and it was diverse from all the beasts that were before it; and it had ten horns. Dan 7:23 Thus he said, The fourth beast shall be the fourth kingdom upon earth, which shall be diverse from all kingdoms, and shall devour the whole earth, and shall tread it down, and break it in pieces. Dan 7:24 And the ten horns out of this kingdom are ten kings that shall arise: and another shall rise after them; and he shall be diverse from the first, and he shall subdue three kings."*

This dreadful and terrible beast, otherwise call the iron monarchy of the World, began under the Caesuras in 168 BC terrorizing the world and destroying all in its path. The ten horns represent the 10 nations of Europe into which the Roman Empire disintegrated, after which a little horn arose. Note the following about the Little Horn.

1.  It came up among the ten horns. It would arise out of Rome.

2.  It came up after the ten horns. After 476 AD which was the breakup of the Roman Empire.

3.  It was different from the first ten- The others were political, but this will be religious.

4.  It would displace three Kingdoms. The papacy destroyed the Heruli, Ostrogoths, and Vandals.

5.  It would have eyes like a man -- Eyes signified divine intelligence, but this was the human eye, signifying it was led by a man who presumes the authority of God.

# THE GLORIES OF ZION

Furthermore the Bible says:

> *Dan 7:25 "And he shall speak great words against the most High, and shall wear out the saints of the most High, and think to change times and laws: and they shall be given into his hand until a time and times and the dividing of time."*

The apostasy of the Christian church would undermine the authority of God. Those who opposed it would be worn out. God's authority is based on His creator ship. He commanded through John in Revelation 14:7.

> *Rev 14:7 "Saying with a loud voice, Fear God, and give glory to him; for the hour of his judgment is come: and worship him that made heaven, and earth, and the sea, and the fountains of waters."*

God is here demanding worship. He demands it on the authority of His law, and the bases of Creation. A man would come along however, that would think to change times and law. God cannot change His law because that is not in His nature, because the Bible states God cannot change

> *Psalm 89:34 "My covenant will I not break, nor alter the things that have gone out of my mouth."*

This little horn would set up a new day in a bid to replace God's day. God did 3 things to the Sabbath when he created it according to Genesis two:

1. He blessed it
2. He rested on it
3. He sanctified it.

Black Citizens of Zion

Since, no man but God can bless or sanctify, this means the 7th Day remains forever blessed and sanctified.

Early in the 2nd Century however, Christians began to celebrate the Crucifixion weekend. They centered this on the day of the Passover, which was the day Christ was crucified. People soon began to associate Christianity with Judaism, so the church decided to celebrate the resurrection instead of the crucifixion.

Sixus, Bishop of the church then instituted the annual resurrection feast. The pagan had been celebrating Sunday for centuries as the Day of the Sun, and they welcomed such a change.

In Ad 200 Pope Victor said all bishops who would not follow the plan of the yearly observance of Easter would be excommunicated. This of course was just his attempt to show his control over the church. Prior to this, the situation was as described below.

> *"Although almost all churches throughout the world celebrate the sacred mysteries on the Sabbath of every week, yet the Christians of Alexandria and Rome on account of some ancient tradition have refused to do this."[9]*

Later in 321 AD Constantine Emperor of Rome and leader of the Church passed the first Sunday law to hold sacred the venerable day of the sun. Things then began to change.

> *"An on the day called Sunday, all who live in the cities or in the country gather together to one place...Sunday is the day on which we all hold our common assembly*

---

[9]General Conference of 7th Day Adventist. Our firm foundation: *A report of the Seventh Day Adventist Bible Conference held September 1-13.1952.* Vol.1 (Washington DC: Review and Herald Publishing Association, 1953), 651.

## THE GLORIES OF ZION

> *because it is the first day on which God made the world; and Jesus Christ our Savior on that same day rose from the dead."*[10]

Rich men who worked on Sunday were fined half their estates, if they continued, they would be made slaves. Servants were flogged and the lower classes banished from the Kingdom.

In the early years of Christianity, Africa flourished as a Christian center. Ethiopia was converted to Judaism during the time of Solomon and they were among the first to accept Christianity. When the world itself, followed Catholicism, and the Crusades and Holy wars raged, there was one nation that was quietly serving God in seclusion. Cut off by Moslems invaders, and fighting for survival, the "Land of the Cushites" vigilantly upheld the gospel of Jesus Christ. J. A Rogers in his book "Great Men of Color," tells the following story.

> *"In AD 330 a number of Phoenicians who were on route to India were shipwrecked off the coast of Ethiopia, among them the two young sons of the leader Merobius. The Ethiopians who were then at war with Rome, killed all except the two lads. These were presented to the king, Abraha, who took them into his household, one of them Frumentius, became tutor of Abraha, the crown prince, whom he won over to Roman Catholicism. After making other converts, Frumentius returned to Constantinople where he was received by the Emperor, Constantine the Great, who was so impressed by his story that he anointed him head of the church. Returning to Ethiopia with his aides, Frumentius established the church with Abraha, who was now king, giving him full support.*

E. G White further comments:

---

[10] Ibid 649.

## Black Citizens of Zion

> *"Beautiful churches were built, and Catholicism was introduced. Other concessions followed. An edict was issued forbidding the observance of the Sabbath under the severest penalty. But Papal tyranny soon became unbearable and war broke out.*
>
> *After a terrible struggle the Romanists were banished from their dominions, and the ancient faith was restored. The churches rejoiced in their freedom, and they never forgot the lesson they had learned concerning the deception, the fanaticism, and the despotic power of Rome."*[11]

Later because of the institution of African slavery the African woke up in America convinced Sunday the first day of the week was God's Sabbath.

Very few people are aware that the slave was never taught about Christ while in slavery. It was witchcraft and voodoo that reigned on the plantation. There were no churches for slaves, and the slave had to go to the church of the slave master and sit on the ground in the back. This was not allowed too often, because the slave master could not afford to have the slave hearing the same sermons as white folks. The slave master would sometimes invite the preacher to the plantation who would tell the slaves that if they obeyed their master and refrain from stealing his hog, then one day God would place them in the great kitchen in heaven, where they would serve their masters with dignity forever.

The knowledge that in Christ there was neither bond nor free would have led to rebellion after rebellion on the plantations. This was the message the slaves heard when a black preacher came to town and gathered them for service. For the most part however, it was not until slavery had ended that the slaves began learning about Jesus and flocked to Christianity in large numbers.

---

[11] White, E. G. *Spirit if Prophecy Vol. 1*. (Mountain View California: Pacific Press Publishing Association), 578.

## THE GLORIES OF ZION

began learning about Jesus and flocked to Christianity in large numbers.

The recently released slaves found preachers moaning from the pulpit, who knew very little of what the Bible had to say, but he knew how to moan. Without realizing they were walking in the wrong path, the people continued in the tradition of their misled leaders, for them the words of Jesus, rings loud and clear, "In vain, do they worship me, teaching for doctrines the commandments of men."

In the new Zion, Sabbath worship will be restored, and all flesh will return to walk in the path of obedience to God.

**Pharaohs of Egypt. Menes and Akhenaton**

Black Citizens of Zion

Very few would argue whether or not the preceding pictures of early Egyptians were not Africans.

# CHAPTER 3

## *EGYPTIAN CITIZENS OF ZION*

*"I will record Rahab and Babylon among those who acknowledge me- Philistia too, and Tyre, along with Cush- and will say, `This one was born in Zion." (Psalm 87:4 NIV)*

The sons of Korah declare that God will record the people of Rahab, (Egypt) Babylon, Philistia, Tyre and Cush (Ethiopia) as citizens of Zion.

The interesting thing which we will show is that all these nations mentioned had black roots. No white nations are mentioned, not because the Sons of Korah believe there will be no white people in future Zion, but they probably knew no white nations. Up until this time, power brokers in the world were black, and all the nations that settled around Palestine were descendants of Ham. Let us take the time to investigate these various nations mentioned, the first of which is Rahab, an epitaph for the black Nation of Egypt.

Egypt, today called "The Arab Republic of Egypt," was once the Glory of the black race. She was the first daughter of Africa, a living tribute to the ability of Africans to build a lasting empire that could withstand all the onslaught of time and armies for nearly 5,000 years.

Egypt is a country which occupies the northeastern corner of Africa. It is actually a part of the Sahara desert, which gets its fertility from the Nile River which carries the wealth of Africa

## Black Citizens of Zion

from the highlands of Ethiopia to the Fertile Crescent called Egypt.

Cairo, Egypt's capital is the largest city in Africa. When Islam came to Africa in the 7th Century, Egypt was one African nation it completely engulfed. The impact of Islam on this city is unbelievable. Today nearly 93% of Egyptians are Sunni Muslims, although there is a Coptic Christian minority. During the 1940's about 80% of the Egyptian people could not read or write, and we will soon discover that the demise of Black Egypt, was the coming of Islam, the Arabs took one of the greatest legacies of the black race and destroyed it.

It is true that the white race occupied Egypt for many years in leadership roles. Alexander the Great built Alexandria, and was buried there, the Romans made it an important part of their Kingdom. The impact of whites upon this African country however, was nothing compared to the impact of Islam.

European scholars have been trying to claim Egypt as their own. They refuse to admit, in spite of all the evidence, that the black race built the first and greatest civilization. They refuse to admit that Africans are responsible for the spread of knowledge, including medicine, astronomy, mathematics, geometry and writing. On the other hand, to the Greek historians, Egypt was considered Ethiopian territory, and her people were considered Ethiopians. Note the following quotations.

> *"According to Homer and Herodotus, the inhabitants of the following territories were Ethiopians: Sudan, Egypt, Arabia, Palestine, Western Asia and India. The only physical difference in these inhabitants was the texture of the hair."*[12]

---

[12] McKissi, Dwight, *Beyond Roots, The search for Blacks in the Bible*. (Wenonah, NJ, Renaissance Productions, 1974) 21.

# EGYPTIAN CITIZENS OF ZION

> *"According to the Bible, and the Historian Josephus, the Empire of Egypt was started by a Son of Ham called Mizraim. The word Mizraim is translated in the Revised Standard Version of the Bible as Egypt, and according to Fausset's Bible Dictionary, published by Zonderman Press, the word Mizraim means: Children of the Sun. Fausset also points out that Egyptians were of a Nigritian origin, and Egyptians did not call themselves Egyptians, this name was later given to them by the Greeks"* [13]

Speaking of Egypt and its people, one author writes:

> *"The Ancient inhabitants of this African land called the country Khem, or Kam, which literally means "the Black land" and they call themselves Khemi or Kamites, or Hamites, meaning the Black people.* [14] 21

> *"The old Egyptian name is Kemi (Copt, Chemi, Keme), which Plutarch says is derived from the ash gray color of the soil covered by the slime of the Nile, but which is more correct to trace to Ham and to regard as indication of the Hametic descent of its first inhabitants".* [15]

Then to confirm the historical data with scientific fact, one author writes:

> *"A melanin test was taken from the skin of an Egyptian Mummy...the melanin proved the Egyptian was Black."* [16]

Of course, for the Christian, the Bible is God's divine word, and cannot lie. Therefore, if the black man can trust no other book, he can trust the Bible. The Bible states, beyond the shadow of

---

[13] Ibid.
[14] McKissi, Dwight, *Beyond Roots, The search for Blacks in the Bible.* (Wenonah, NJ, Renaissance Productions, 1974), 21.
[15] Ibid 22.
[16] Ibid 21.

a doubt, that Egypt was considered a part of the land of Ham, which means, its people were Black. Please note.

> *Psalm 78:51 "And smote all the firstborn in Egypt; the chief of their strength in the tabernacles of Ham:"*

> *Psalm 105:23 "Israel also came into Egypt; and Jacob sojourned in the land of Ham."*

> *Psalm 105:27 "They shewed his signs among them, and wonders in the land of Ham."*

> *Psalm 106:22 "Wondrous works in the land of Ham, and terrible things by the Red sea."*

Speaking as to the color of the descendants of Ham, one author wrote:

> *"The word Ham is derived from the Egyptian Kam which is the strongest word in the language for Black or Blackness. It means dark or Black and he is regarded as the father of Negroes, Mongoloids and Indians"* [17]

Moses of course was educated in Egypt, and used this education to write the first five books of the Bible.

## MENES

It was the great king Menes who first united what was known as Upper and Lower Egypt under one government. During one of the longest reigns in history, Menes brought stability to Egypt. He set the ground work for Egypt to spread its wings and become one of the greatest and most enduring empires to ever exist in the history of the world. It was this Black king who later gave Egypt its name when the Greeks called the city of

---

[17] McKissi, Dwight, *Beyond Roots, The search for Blacks in the Bible.* (Wenonah, NJ, Renaissance Productions, 1974), 21.

## EGYPTIAN CITIZENS OF ZION

Memphis "Aigyptos." Speaking as to its grandeur, one scholar writes:

> *"Like Ur and Akkad, Memphis was a glittering city of untold splendor, and unrivaled center of civilization; although it had the disadvantage, like Sumer and Akkad of lying in the midst of lands which could hardly have been more ill disposed or envious."* [18]

Mene's power was limited in the development stage of his kingship, but by the 3rd dynasty, royal power had greatly increased and massive pyramids sprang up where the Pharaohs were laid to rest.

Recognizing what was happening to Egypt, and desiring to share in the wealth of this glorious black nation, the Asiatic race began to flood into Egypt from all directions. This posed a serious threat to the survival of Egypt's black power and the Africans were forced to act.

> *"To counter this ever present threat, it was necessary for the Egyptians to extend military operations far beyond the line now marked by the Suez Canal, and this they did not fail to do. They safeguarded the Isthmus of Suez itself by means of the wall of the Prince, one of the world's first iron curtains, of which a priest wrote about in 2650 BC: "the wall of the Prince is being built to keep the Asians out of Egypt" Beyond this fortification were Egyptian outposts which commanded the whole Red Sea coast of the Sinai peninsula, and in particular the southern tip with its rich copper and jewel mines."* [19]

Internal strength encouraged expansion and aggression abroad. The Egyptians had extensive trade contracts with

---

[18] Herm, Gerhard, *The Phoenicians*, (Williams Morrow and Company Inc. New York, 1975), 22.

[19] Herm, Gerhard, *The Phoenicians*, (Williams Morrow and Company Inc. New York, 1975), 22.

Black Citizens of Zion

Syria, Palestine, and northeast Africa. They pushed into the Sinai and northern Nubia, areas at that time like Egypt, dominated by a Negro race.

By the 4th and 5th dynasties, Egyptian armies were raiding Palestine and southern Nubia. This expansionist activity was reduced by the 6th dynasty however, as regional kingdoms became stronger, and Egypt became defensive.

The powerful 11 through 12 Theban Dynasty soon brought Egypt back to its glorious days, and exercised strong leadership. The days of plenty were not to last forever however, and just before the collapse of Black power, Jacob and his family moved into Egypt to find refuge from a famine that attacked their land.

## ISRAEL

Joseph the youngest son of Jacob had been sold to the black Midianites who were on their way to Africa to carry on trade with their brothers in Egypt. While in Egypt, Joseph became the second in command because of his wisdom in saving the Egyptians from starvation during a severe famine, as a reward he was given a new name and an African wife by the name of Asenath. This Egyptian was to bear Joseph two sons, Manasseh and Ephraim. These boys though Africans were later numbered among the twelve tribes of Israel. It was their African descendants, who would later march out of Egypt under the banner of these two tribes. The Bible states:

> *GENESIS 41:50" And unto Joseph were born two sons before the years of famine came, which Asenath the daughter of Poti-pherah priest of on bare unto him. GENESIS 41:51 And Joseph called the name of the firstborn Manasseh: For God, said he, hath made me forget all my toil, and all my father's house. GENESIS 41:52 And the name of the second called he Ephraim: For God hath caused me to be fruitful in the land of my affliction."*

# EGYPTIAN CITIZENS OF ZION

These events opened the door for Jacob and his other sons to go to Egypt. There they were given the best land and became a powerful force in Egypt. The twelfth Dynasty in Egypt, rolled out the red carpet for the Children of Israel.

## MIDIANITES

The Midianites were responsible for saving Joseph from death at the hands of his brothers, by purchasing him as a slave. The brothers of Joseph did not like him because he was the favorite of their father. Rather than killing him however, the decided to sell him into slavery.

These Midianites, who purchased Joseph, were descendants of Abraham and his black wife Ketura. They worshipped Yahweh just as the Jews did. Jethro their leader, the father-in-law of Moses, was responsible for the organization of Israel into a cohesive nation.

It was while living among Jethro and his people that Moses was introduced to Horeb, "The Mount of God." This was Midianites territory and they themselves probably spoke with God on many occasions on this very mountain. Moses found himself among these people after having been banished from Egypt for killing an Egyptian. While there in the mountains of Midian, Moses wrote the book of Genesis. No doubt his black father-in-law was a tremendous source of information as Moses researched the history of mankind and the creation of the world. Jethro was probably responsible for the full details of the sale of Joseph to the Egyptian, although Moses must have learnt this earlier from his people while living in Egypt.

Everything Moses knew, he learnt from the Africans. He was educated in the African schools of Egypt in chivalry and science, and later he learned about the God of the Jews from an aged African named Jethro. This God Yahweh would later command Moses to leave the Midianites and go back to the Continent of the Motherland to liberate his people.

## Black Citizens of Zion

When the Israelites left Egypt, Moses invited the Black Midianites to go with him and his people as they traveled to the Promised Land. He assured the Midianites that God would be with them and give them the same blessing He promised the Hebrews. Some of the Midianites did go with Moses as scouts. They knew well the terrain of the land, and were of the same skin color as the Canaanites who lived in the land of Palestine.

The Midianites were later called Kenites. They settled with the children of Judah and their descendants were a part of the crowds to whom Jesus preached while on earth. Moses the liberator of the Hebrews took his wife from among these people.

Trouble came to Egypt during the closing years of the 12th dynasty. The mighty Black kings were now replaced by the Hyksos and two centuries of disaster and decay was to follow. Phoenicia became a dominant world power free of Egypt, and reached its zenith when the Hittites arrived. The Egyptian monarchs preoccupied with internal problems, could not protect their vassal states. Phoenicia was to become a black kingdom that was to be one of the richest empires that ever existed.

Egypt stood divided. Thebes became the stronghold of Blacks who did not desire intermarriage and mixture with the Causation and Asiatic races which began to invade Egypt. The country was now ruled by three Pharaohs: king Amoses, who sat on the throne, the Hyksos and the Cushites in Thebes.

Before long, the black capital of Thebe became the Mother of cities. She developed massive armies, proud fearless warriors and magnificent temples. The temples became known as Universities and centers of learning where the highest standard of excellence was encouraged. This led to the development of art, writing and mathematics, which came about because of the need to record and calculate the massive wealth of the priesthood.

Eventually expelling the Hyksos, the Theban insurgents founded the 18th dynasty. This dynasty inaugurated ancient

# EGYPTIAN CITIZENS OF ZION

Egypt's most brilliant period. It was called by historians and Egyptologists, "The New kingdom." The Pharaohs of this dynasty were some of the greatest to ever rule Egypt, Hatshepsut, Thutmose III, Akhenaten, Seti and Ramses 11 expanded Egypt's territory more than ever before. Strong government evolved, and the worship of the Pharaohs became elaborate. Their armies marched across the Sudan, Palestine and Asia. Vassal kings were propped up, respect and adoration were offered by all of Egypt's neighbors along with the other powers who were trying to wrest some of Egypt's territory from her hands.

Egypt again was a world empire. The eastern Mediterranean and western Asia were now within the borders of this African kingdom. Diop writes:

> *"In total, according to Thutmose III Hymn of Triumph, written in verse engraved on the "poetic stele" at Karnak, facing Thebes in Upper Egypt, foreign states were conquered and integrated to different degrees into the Egyptian empire. In one year, under Thutmose III, the Egyptian treasury collected 3,500 kilos of gold (Electrum), of which nine-tenths came from the tributes paid by vassals. Western Asia was divided into administrative districts placed under the authority of Egyptian governors, charged with collecting the tributes, or annual taxes, that all these defeated and vassal states had to pay to the Egyptian treasury."*[20]
>
> *"In some towns, as in Jaffa, the conquered princes were purely and simply replaced by Egyptian generals, and the administration was direct. Whereas Thutmose III discharged the conquered chief of the town of Aleppo, in Syria, he replaced him with another vassal "On whom he conferred sovereignty in ceremony of investiture by, anointing him with oil," according to the Egyptian custom which Christianity would take over on a different*

---

[20] Diop, Cheikh Anta, *Civilization or Barbarism* (NY: Lawrence Hill Books, 1991 Edition: 1st edition), 85.

# Black Citizens of Zion

*level. These conquered states kept small territorial guards trained by the Egyptian officers. But the defense of this huge empire rested on the Egyptian army itself, so much so that, even under Amenophis III, the Phoenician towns would protest when they felt the Egyptian troops in charge of their protection were insufficient. Egyptian garrisons were stationed at strategic points, important towns and ports; the vassal chief of the country of the Amorites was authorized to organize a small defensive army. Fourteen hundred years before Rome, Egypt created the first centralized empire in the world"*[21]

## THE EXODUS

The Eighteenth dynasty was the dynasty of the Exodus. It was while the Thebans ruled that Moses was born and abandoned on the Nile River by his parents in an attempt to save His life. Eventually the daughter of the Pharaoh was to draw him from the Nile, and named him Moses. After being trained in the schools of Egypt, the child drawn from the Nile received a call from God while living in the mountains of Median. He would return to Egypt to lead His people from slavery to freedom.

According to the book of Numbers, there were at least 72,000 families of pure African descent in the massive crowd awaiting the command of the Lord to cross over Jordan. They were descendants of Ephraim and Manasseh. Further-more, there was the largest section of the crowd known as the mixed multitude, Black Egyptians who had married into this Hebrew race, or had been converted into the Hebrew religion, Then there were the Black in-laws of Moses, who were mentioned earlier in this chapter.

## JOSHUA

It was a descendant of the African woman Asenath that was to lead the Children of Israel across the Jordan River, and into the

---
[21] Ibid 85.

## EGYPTIAN CITIZENS OF ZION

Promised Land. His name was Joshua, Son of Nun, born of the African tribe of Ephraim, a Black man of energy, push and tremendous enterprise.

For forty years he had shared the slavery and sorrow of a captive people. His childish eyes had witnessed the brutality of the Egyptian taskmasters. It is highly possible Joshua's shoulder was never torn by the cruel whips of his brothers. This is likely because Joshua according to Egyptian custom belonged to family of the African Priest. Furthermore, since he figures prominently in the freedom movement, he was probably never a slave. Joshua beholding the condition of his people might have felt compelled to do something to affect their freedom. The Egyptians like the African of the 18th Century who sold his brother for riches, were spelling the demise of the African Continent by their treatment of the Hebrews.

Joshua was on the mount when God invited Moses to come up and receive the table of stones on which God had written the Ten Commandments with his own fingers. He stood by when, like a devouring fire, God appeared upon the mountain. For forty days and forty nights, God communicated with Moses and Joshua as he had with few men before.

The land to which God was leading his people was "Black Man's Country." It was Canaan, home of the giants, an area belonging to the Sons of Ham, who were brothers to Nimrod. In this country lived military geniuses. They settled here because it was the cross roads of the world and they alone had proved to be militarily able to withstand the onslaught that living in Palestine required.

Canaan was Black man's country, cities strongly fortified- Jericho, Ai, Gilgal, Jerusalem, Hebron, Lachish, Eglon, Jarmoth. Cities that stood as a monument to the ability of the Black race to build structures of magnificence and beauty. Peace and tranquility existed within their walls. They built mountainous fortresses and strongholds that would defy any power in those days.

## Black Citizens of Zion

The Canaanites were a powerful people, fierce and warlike. Armed and ready to stop any intruder, any nation ready to claim Palestine as theirs. They had horsemen, and chariots, and instruments of war, of which Israel had none.

These Children of Ham were empire builders. Before Joshua was Jericho, behind him Egypt. These were Black empires, built by the sweat of their brows, with the strength of their hands. They feared no one thus far, but Yahweh was with Joshua, and a fearless African, and a powerful God, was too much for any people. Read the words of Yahweh to His people:

> *Isaiah 41:10 "Fear thou not; for I am with thee: be not dismayed; for I am thy God: I will strengthen thee; yea, I will help thee; yea, I will uphold thee with the right hand of my righteousness."*
>
> *Joshua 1:3-6 3 "Every place that the sole of your foot shall tread upon, that have I given unto you, as I said unto Moses. 4 From the wilderness and this Lebanon even unto the great river, the river Euphrates, all the land of the Hittites, and unto the great sea toward the going down of the sun, shall be your coast. 5 There shall not any man be able to stand before thee all the days of thy life: as I was with Moses, so I will be with thee: I will not fail thee, nor forsake thee. 6 Be strong and of a good courage: for unto this people shalt thou divide for an inheritance the land, which I swear unto their fathers to give."*

All through the arduous campaign that followed, nothing could daunt Joshua's courage. This man of African descent had learnt that as long as Yahweh was on his side, there was nothing to fear. This is a lesson that men of African descent must learn the world over if we are to survive the difficult days ahead. We must learn to sing:

> *"Guide me Oh thou great Jehovah*
> *Pilgrim through this barren land.*

## EGYPTIAN CITIZENS OF ZION

*I am weak but thou art mighty*
*Lead me with thy powerful hand.*
*Bread of Heaven, Feed me, till I want no more.*

*When I tread the verge of Jordan*
*Bid my anxious fear subside*
*Death of death and hell's destruction*
*Land me safe on Canaan side"*

The people of Israel and the people of Canaan were to inhabit the land together. They co-existed until they blended into one people.

After Joshua and his people left Egypt, eventually the country fell to the Cushites or Ethiopians, whose 25th dynasty brought unity and resisted Assyrian expansion into Syria-Palestine. Egypt spends her last glorious days as part of the Nation of Ethiopia when the Africans sought to take back their land from the Asians who ruled Egypt from 715 BC. Shabaka, Piankhi and Taharqa proved as formidable foes for the Assyrians who were now laying claim to Egypt. But when Ashurbanipal invaded Egypt in 669 BC, the militant Blacks gave up Egypt, resulting in the domination of the Black populace who remained behind in their hometown. A new Black Empire was now established in Ethiopia, the new Black stronghold, of what was later to be called Africa. The land of the Burnt face, or the Billad of Sudan, "Home of the Blacks."

Egypt, the greatest achievement of the Black race had fallen, but her teachings and history were accepted by Judaism and then Christianity, and so her heritage still lives.

## EGYPTIAN TEACHINGS

The concept of the Triune God was first taught by Egypt. This probably came from the Garden of Eden, but it first appeared among this African people. They taught about heaven, hell and life after death. The Egyptians taught that one was required to live a moral life or find themselves in the furnace of hell. Interestingly enough, this furnace was guarded by a serpent.

The Egyptian believed and taught the concept of the "Great Controversy" between good and evil. They presented God and the evil serpent fighting daily for control of the earth, with God always being victorious.

The virgin birth of the Savior was an Egyptian concept and the very images of Mary and Jesus when they first appeared were the image of an African woman and her son.

In mathematics, the Pythagoras theory and Archimedes principles were being used on the African continent long before either Greek men were born after whom these principles were named, as is brought out by the Papyrus of Moscow. It many cases, It can clearly be demonstrated that many Greek and Roman achievements were simply a copy of what the Africans had already accomplished in math and science.

These Africans had knowledge of steel production and the very word chemistry was derived from their word Kemit, which means Black, alluding to the long cooking process used in Egypt to extract various elements.

The Egyptians were an ingenious people and one can sympathize with the European scholars who try to make them white in this age of bigotry and racial intolerance. The Bible is clear however, that they were Hametic, and when we get to heaven, the Sons of Egypt will be there as, "Black Citizens of Zion."

# CHAPTER 4

## *BABYLONIAN CITIZENS OF ZION*

*GENESIS 10:1 "Now these are the generations of the sons of Noah, Shem, Ham, and Japheth: and unto them were sons born after the flood. 10:6 And the sons of Ham; Cush, and Mizraim, and Phut, and Canaan. 10:7 And the sons of Cush; Seba, and Havilah, and Sabtah, and Raamah, and Sabtecha: and the sons of Raamah; Sheba, and Dedan. 10:8 And Cush begat Nimrod: he began to be a mighty one in the earth. 10:9 He was a mighty hunter before the LORD: wherefore it is said, Even as Nimrod the mighty hunter before the LORD. 10:10 And the beginning of his kingdom was Babel, and Erech, and Accad, and Calneh, in the land of Shinar."*

Babylon, In the Semitic Tongue, 'Babilu,' meaning "The gate of God" was the second greatest Black empire to rule the world.

Babylon began before recorded history at the time of the Tower of Babel by Nimrod. Nimrod a grandson of Ham was its first leader. He was a hunter of great strength and power, one who could match Samson in his physical prowess, and far exceeding that Hebrew judge in intellectual genius. This Nimrod decided he would protect his people from another flood, by establishing a tower that reached into heaven.

After the destruction of the earth by a universal flood, Nimrod gathered the descendants of Noah. Under the leadership of this great Black monarch, men of Color, Caucasoid and Semitic origins banded together to build the highest tower the world had ever known. Babel was the beginning of the kingdom of Babylon.

This great hunter Nimrod, according to the historian Josephus:

> *"Persuaded the citizens who he ruled to worship him as God and to look to his strength to guide them and not Yahweh who had just destroyed the world with a flood. He said he would revenge Himself on God, he would build a tower that would stretch high into the heavens, into the very presence of God so that should Yahweh decide to destroy the world with another flood, he and his people would not be affected.."*[22]

God, on recognizing that the sons of men were about to accomplish their task, intervened. He confounded their language which was universal at that time. They could no longer understand each other, so they were forced to migrate into different people, grouped according their language. Thus began a multitude of nations, and Nimrod's purpose was defeated.

It is reported that Nimrod saw himself as the son of Baal. He was aware of the promise God made to put enmity between the serpent and the seed of the woman in Genesis 3:15. Every generation since Eve diligently looked for the birth of the man child. This child was to restore the relationship between the children of Adam and the Triune Godhead that created them.

Nimrod developed a society that would challenge even one in 20th Century America. He built a city that was enduring with a tremendous list of kings. For nearly 2,000 years Babylon was to the capital of an extensive empire called Babylonia. Its first documented king was Sargon of Akkad. He was one of the most powerful kings to ever rule any nation. Sargon,

---

[22] Josephus, Flavious, *Antiquities of the Jews* (London, Printed for J. Cooke, No. 17, Pater-noster-Row, [1785-1786] ), 32

# BABYLONIAN CITIZENS OF ZION

> *"Dreamt of an empire that would stretch from Anatolia to the Nile valley, where there would be no national differences, only citizens with the same rules, the same statue and the same rights, who would look submissively toward his glorious capital"*[23]

Sargon was the most famous of the early kings of Babylonia. He ruled for 56 years conquering many neighboring countries, and was responsible for adding Sumer or Mesopotamia to the Babylonian kingdom. After Sargon came Naram Sin, who conquered a large part of Western Asia, establishing Babylon's power in Palestine and even stretching its arm into the Siniatic peninsula.

Hammurabi was the next most famous king of Babylon. He came to the throne right after the Patriarch Abraham was called out of Ur of the Chaldees, one of the cities of Babylon. Under him, the first golden age of Babylon began. Hammarabi was a genius politician who loved scholarly and literary pursuit. His most enduring legacy was a code of laws fashioned after the Ten Commandments. These laws were found carved on a column at Susa in the palace of the Assyrians. The Assyrians were the leaders of Babylon until Nabopolassar, the father of Nebuchadnezzar, set his people free.

According to the Seventh day Adventist Bible Commentary, Nebuchadnezzar came to the throne in 605 BC. His father, Nabopolassar, was founder of the new Chaldean dynasty in Babylonia. It was this dynasty which restored Black rule after the foreign rulers were overthrown.

Nabopolassar was appointed by the Assyrians as governor of Babylon. In 626 he revolted and joined the Medes and Persians in a war against Assyria which resulted in the destruction of the Assyrian capital of Nineveh in 612 BC. After driving the last Assyrians into northwestern Mesopotamia, Nabopolassar left military operations in the hands of his son

---

[23]Ibid 51.

Black Citizens of Zion

Nebuchadnezzar. Nebuchadnezzar then dispersed the Assyrians, pushed their Egyptian allies out of Syria, and was about to invade Egypt itself when he received news of his father's death. He then returned home to Babylon to assume the throne of is people.

Nebuchadnezzar ruled Babylon some 4,000 years after Nimrod, yet he continued in the tradition of the founder of his great empire. Nebuchadnezzar regarded himself as the Messiah, and king of all kings. It was his plan like Nimrod, to set up a kingdom that would be universal and include all the people of the world, this task he nearly accomplished. Note the following about Nebuchadnezzar's kingdom.

> *"The inhabitants of His kingdom lived in solidly built villas of thirteen or fourteen rooms, walked on broad well paved streets, divided up the day into twenty four hours of sixty minutes, were able to read and write and even had trouble with their tax returns,"*[24]

In Babylonia, but most conspicuously in Babylon itself, Nebuchadnezzar engaged in numerous building projects. He fortified Babylon constructing many temples and the great Hanging Gardens.

Nebuchadnezzar took a Midianite woman to be his wife. This was the Black tribe from which the prophet Moses took his spouse. These Midianites lived in the beautiful mountains of Midian and loved the natural scenes. Nebuchadnezzar to keep His lovely Black woman happy built her the beautiful "Hanging Gardens of Babylon," trees and flowers built on top of a platform 23 feet high, visible from miles around. These hanging gardens were later numbered among the Seven Wonders of the World. Speaking of Nebuchadnezzar's achievements, Ellen G. White wrote.

---

[24] Herm, Gerhard *The Phoenicians* (Williams Morrow and Company Inc. New York 1975), 21.

## BABYLONIAN CITIZENS OF ZION

> *"It was given Nebuchadnezzar's lot, after years of patient and wearing labor, to conquer Tyre; Egypt and Judah. He added nation after nation to the Babylonian realm and added more and more to His fame as the greatest ruler of the age.[25]*
> *It is not surprising that this successful monarch, so ambitious and so proud spirited, should be tempted to turn aside from the path of humility, which alone leads to true greatness. "[26]*

The nation of Israel, thinking Egypt would continued to be great, sided with the African kingdom against Babylon. Nebuchadnezzar then marched against Judah, destroyed their capital and took their sons and daughters captive. Included among these captives was Daniel, author of the book named after him in the Old Testament Scripture. For 35 years these captives were a witness to Nebuchadnezzar. Daniel especially prayed with and for the king. This Black king and his Hebrew subject shared a remarkably close relationship.

Through the years of their Babylonian captivity, Daniel and his friends witnessed to Nebuchadnezzar, revealing the principles of the true God. God worked patiently on the mind of this young Black king, but it would take supernatural intervention to bring him to acknowledge Yahweh as his God.

Daniel was 18 when he was taken into captivity. By the time Nebuchadnezzar was converted in Chapter 4 of the Book of Daniel, Daniel was 53 years old. He lived in captivity for 35 years, patiently working on the mind and heart of this king who resisted God's claim upon his life for many years.

Nebuchadnezzar resisted God for 35 years. He saw the superiority of Daniel's wisdom and faithfulness; he was aware that Daniel's God was superior to his own and had the ability to

---

[25] White, Ellen *Prophets & Kings* (Mountain View California, Pacific Press Publishing Association), 515.
[26] Ibid

## Black Citizens of Zion

reveal the future. His eyes had beheld God in the burning fiery furnace when the three Hebrew boys were thrown there for refusing to bow down to Nebuchadnezzar's golden image. Yet God had to do something drastic to get the attention of Nebuchadnezzar. Consider the following passage:

> *DAN 4:5 "I saw a dream which made me afraid, and the thoughts upon my bed and the visions of my head troubled me. 4:6 Therefore made I a decree to bring in all the wise men of Babylon before me, that they might make known unto me the interpretation of the dream. 4:7 Then came in the magicians, the astrologers, the Chaldeans, and the soothsayers: and I told the dream before them; but they did not make known unto me the interpretation thereof."*

Nebuchadnezzar had everything his heart desired. For him, it was a time of great prosperity and popularity. He not only lived in the most powerful nation on earth at the time, but he was king of the capital of the world. Armies marched at his command and cities feared his wrath. He was rich, powerful and built the greatest city that ever existed up until that time.

Then one day he had a dream that brought fear to his heart, and troubled his life. He quickly made a decree that the wise men of Babylon should be brought to interpret the dream, but they failed him. He then called for Daniel who had proved himself before, and Daniel revealed to the king the meaning of the dream after consulting with God.

The Dream of Nebuchadnezzar:

> *"10 Thus were the visions of mine head in my bed; I saw, and behold a tree in the midst of the earth, and the height thereof was great. 11 The tree grew, and was strong, and the height thereof reached unto heaven, and the sight thereof to the end of all the earth: 12 The leaves thereof were fair, and the fruit thereof much, and in it was meat for all: the beasts of the field had*

# BABYLONIAN CITIZENS OF ZION

*shadow under it, and the fowls of the heaven dwelt in the boughs thereof, and all flesh was fed of it. 13 I saw in the visions of my head upon my bed, and, behold, a watcher and an holy one came down from heaven; 14 He cried aloud, and said thus, Hew down the tree, and cut off his branches, shake off his leaves, and scatter his fruit: let the beasts get away from under it, and the fowls from his branches: 15 Nevertheless leave the stump of his roots in the earth, even with a band of iron and brass, in the tender grass of the field; and let it be wet with the dew of heaven, and let his portion be with the beasts in the grass of the earth: 16 Let his heart be changed from man's, and let a beast's heart be given unto him; and let seven times pass over him. 17 This matter is by the decree of the watchers, and the demand by the word of the holy ones: to the intent that the living may know that the most High ruleth in the kingdom of men, and giveth it to whomsoever he will, and setteth up over it the basest of men." (Daniel 4:10-17)*

## The Meaning of the Dream

*"24 This is the interpretation, O king, and this is the decree of the most High, which is come upon my lord the king: 25 That they shall drive thee from men, and thy dwelling shall be with the beasts of the field, and they shall make thee to eat grass as oxen, and they shall wet thee with the dew of heaven, and seven times shall pass over thee, till thou know that the most High ruleth in the kingdom of men, and giveth it to whomsoever he will. 26 And whereas they commanded to leave the stump of the tree roots; thy kingdom shall be sure unto thee, after that thou shalt have known that the heavens do rule. 27 Wherefore, O king, let my counsel be acceptable unto thee, and break off thy sins by righteousness, and thine iniquities by shewing*

## Black Citizens of Zion

> *mercy to the poor; if it may be a lengthening of thy tranquility."(Daniel 4:24-27)*

It is unfortunate that God must sometimes use catastrophe to cause men to come to their senses. Nebuchadnezzar was on a course to eternal ruin, and God realize unless He did something drastic, the great king would not be saved. God therefore caused a disease the doctors call Lycanthropy to come upon Him. According to the medical dictionary, it is temporary insanity that comes suddenly and is completely reversible, and sometimes goes away as quickly as it comes.(Mark Finley, Lectures on Daniel 4)

Daniel loved Nebuchadnezzar. He loved the king that had destroyed his homeland and kept him enslaved for 35 years. Daniel pleaded with him, "Nebuchadnezzar, change you course -- accept God today and He will spare you."

I think the attitude of Daniel toward his oppressor is an attitude all men and women of African descent must take toward the race that enslaved us and still oppresses us today. Hate will only destroy us. Love is the most powerful force in the universe and it has the ability to heal many wounds and bind many broken relationships.

Despite Daniel's love for him, Nebuchadnezzar was too proud to admit that all he had accomplished was because the God of Israel had allowed it. Twelve months later he walked out of his palace and looked at all the luxury and glory he had acquired.

Picture this massive Black genius, who stands almost like a giant, surveying the extensive golden empire he now ruled. He thinks of his ancestry, the great Black kings that had ruled before him. He reflects on the massive libraries of Sargon discovered by archaeologists, and the great laws of Hammarabi laid down during the time of Abraham.

Before Nebuchadnezzar walked the Black people of Babylon, proud of their heritage and achievement in writing and literature. They won some tremendous battles, only 50 years

## BABYLONIAN CITIZENS OF ZION

before Babylon had been under the influence of the Assyrians when Nebuchadnezzar and his father destroyed the City of Nineveh. Now the only great threat to his empire was his Black brothers in Egypt and Phoenicia.

There was rest around the nation of Babylon. Its massive walls according to the historian Herodotus was 85 feet thick and 340 feet High. Chariots could be seen traveling the massive structure which stood on the Euphrates which flowed through its midst and divided it into two almost equal parts. (As quoted by Mark Finley in Lectures on Daniel 4)

Standing before Nebuchadnezzar was the magnificent hanging gardens. They were loaded with golden ornaments and trinkets. These gardens are named among the Seven Wonders of the World, monuments which like the Ziggurats of Egypt depicted the intellectual genius of the Black race who were the architects and builders of these massive structures.

Babylon was the largest of all ancient capitals with its walls, according to the historian Herodotus, stretching for fifty-five miles. The city had 53 temples, 955 sanctuaries and 384 altars all in a 14 mile radius. The following words were discovered by archaeologists while excavating Babylon

> *"O Babylon, whosoever beholds thee is filled with rejoicing,*
> *Whosoever dwells in Babylon increases his life,*
> *Whosoever speaks evil of Babylon is like one who kills his own mother. Babylon is like a sweet date palm, whose fruit is lovely to behold."*[27]

When the inner palace of Nebuchadnezzar was discovered by archaeologists, they found statues and inscriptions of Babylon's glorious past, all there to use the words of Nebuchadnezzar, for all men to behold his greatness.

---

[27] Nichol, Francis D., *The Seventh-day Adventist Bible Commentary*, (Washington, D.C.: Review and Herald Publishing Association) 1978.

## Black Citizens of Zion

The following words were discovered when Babylon was excavated:

> "I have made Babylon the Holy city, the glory of the great God's more prominent than before.....No king among all kings has ever created, no earlier king has ever build, what I have magnificently build...
>
> All my valuable works, the beautification of the sanctuaries, of the great God's which I undertook more than my royal ancestors, I wrote in a document and put it down for coming generations... May the way of my life be long may I rejoice in offspring, May my offspring rule over the Black headed people into all eternity, may the mention of my name be proclaim for good at all future times."[28]

Nebuchadnezzar saw before him the massive 90 feet Golden Statue he had build, his armies posted on the walls, his beautiful Black women bathing by the pool and his children in the garden. This caused his heart to be lifted up. It was then that this tower of a Black man, this descendant of Ham, brother of the burnt face Sons of Cush, raised his outstretched arms, dressed in his regal robe, his Babylonian gown reaching down to his feet, his massive crown with golden diadems, rubies and pearls resting smugly on his kinky hair now turning gray, ascribes all his greatness to himself, and declares:

> "Is not this great Babylon I have built as the royal residence, by my mighty power and for the glory of my majesty?" (Daniel 4:30)

Immediately God intervened and commanded to the Angel Gabriel:

---

[28] Nichol, Francis D., *The Seventh-day Adventist Bible Commentary*, Vol. 4, (Washington, D.C.: Review and Herald Publishing Association, 1978) 799.

## BABYLONIAN CITIZENS OF ZION

> *"Take his kingdom; drive him from the haunts of men. Make him dwell with the beast of the field; let his hair grow like that of an eagle feather and his nails like the claws of a bird. Let Him eat grass as an ox for seven years, until he understands the Most High God rules in the kingdom of men. Teach this towering Black giant what all men, Black and white must learn through the centuries to come; the most High God rules in the courts of men, He sets up Kings, takes down Kings, and gives a kingdom to whomever he chooses."*

Nebuchadnezzar was taken from the throne. For seven years he lost his mind. Like an animal he wondered upon the earth until he came to his senses, recognizing God has a claim on the life of every man, and he holds us accountable for our actions. Nebuchadnezzar then said:

> *"DAN 4:34 And at the end of the days I Nebuchadnezzar lifted up mine eyes unto heaven, and mine understanding returned unto me, and I blessed the most High, and I praised and honored him that liveth for ever, whose dominion is an everlasting dominion, and his kingdom is from generation to generation."*

When seven years had past and the end had come, Nebuchadnezzar came to his senses and recognized the true God. He prayerfully looked to heaven and God elevated him from the condition of brute beast and restored him to the image of God.

The God of the Bible is still in the business of restoring men today. Listen to the words of the Bible.

> *2 Corinthians 5:17 "Therefore if any man be in Christ, he is a new creature: old things are passed away; behold, all things are become new."*

## Black Citizens of Zion

The Bible is clear that God is still taking men who are behaving like beast and recreating them in His image. Murderers, pimps, and prostitutes it makes no difference. God has the power to make them new. He alone can remove from men the hungriness they feel for the substance that dries up their bodies and destroys their brain. He can take away the loneliness that causes us to give our bodies to one who is neither husband nor wife, desecrating His holy temple. He can give peace in the midst of a troubled world and bring us to our senses just as he did for Nebuchadnezzar, if only we would recognize Him as king of their lives.

This proud Black man whose desire was that his descendants always rule over his people, came to his senses and recognized himself no more as King of Kings, but a subject of Yahweh. Every Black person must come to that point in his life where he realizes that without God he is lost.

This was the realization of our ancestors as they suffered on the slave ships in conditions inhumane and disgraceful. Our women were raped by the slave masters. They found no place to run or hide, yet they found comfort in the shadow of His wings and would sing.

> *"Ain't got long to be here, bound for the Promised Land.*
> *Ain't got long to be here, a got a ticket in my hand.*
> *And when I look around and see troubles all around,*
> *Ain't got time to pay no mind, for I ain't got long to*
> *stay."*

And when the sun scorched their Black skins, and the half-dressed mothers walked with their babies on their backs. When they found no time for rest or refreshment in the cotton fields or on the plantations, when their feet grew hardened and sore, from its bareness upon the hot ground, they sang:

> *"I've got a shoe you got a shoe*
> *All of God's children got a shoe.*

# BABYLONIAN CITIZENS OF ZION

*When I get to heaven I am going to put on my shoe, I am going to walk all over God's heaven."*

This can still be our song if we place our trust in God.

Nebuchadnezzar came to his senses, and one author writes.

> *"The once proud monarch became a humble child of God; the tyrannical overbearing ruler, a wise and compassionate king. He, who had defied and blasphemed the God of heaven, now acknowledges the power of the Most High and earnestly sought to promote the fear of Yahweh and the happiness of His subjects. Under the rebuke of Him who is king of kings and Lord of lords. Nebuchadnezzar had learned at last the lesson which all rulers need to learn."*[29]

Finally, the great Black king surrendered to Yahweh. After his death his empire deteriorated. Twenty-three years later while Nabonidus partied, enjoying wine, women, and song like so many of our African brothers today, Cyrus the Persian took over Babylon without a fight. The second greatest Black empire had ended. Babylon was no more ruled by Black men. But the Bible says, the people of Babylon would be numbered as citizens of the kingdom, they will be there in Zion, "Black Citizens of Zion."

---

[29] White, E. G. *Prophets and Kings* (Mountain View California: Pacific Press Publishing Association), 521.

Black Citizens of Zion

Portion of the Stele containing the Laws of Hammarabi. These laws were similar to the 10 Commandments of the Old Testament scripture.

# CHAPTER 5

## *TYRIAN OR PHOENICIAN CITIZENS OF ZION*

*"And the sons of Ham; Cush, and Mizraim, and Phut, and Canaan. 5 And Canaan begat Sidon his firstborn, and Heth," (Genesis 10:6 & 15)*

Tyre was one of the Phoenician cities which along with Byblos, Sidon and later Carthage were most popular. According to the historian Josephus, the Phoenicians, were a Hametic race which means they were of Black descent. This is also attested to in the Old Testament scriptures as is noted in the above verse.

Sidon was the first son of Canaan and grandson of Ham, father of the Black race. He was responsible for the formation of the first city of Phoenicia called Zidon. His descendants later ruled the coastline of Palestine and started many colonies the main one of which was Carthage.

Tarsus, the hometown of the Apostle Paul, was also Phoenician territory. When one considers that Paul was at times mistaken for an Egyptian (Acts 21:38) this tends to suggest that Paul was a Black man. It is obvious that Paul could not be immediately distinguished as a Jew. This is best recognized in Paul's emphasis that he attended school at Jerusalem, sat at the feet of the great Jewish scholars, and was Hebrew of a Hebrew. The Jewish people were surprised that the apostle spoke Hebrew on one occasion. If Paul was a recognizable Jew, why were they surprised? This leads to the conclusion that Paul looked like a Phoenician, who looked like Africans.

"The Phoenicians called themselves Canaanites even when Alexander took Tyre and were the first people to develop an alphabet with letters form A to Z. The Greeks learnt the alphabet from them and called the alphabet Phoinikia grammar.

Archaeologists have discovered that the Phoenicians wore the same dress and Jewelry as their African brothers in Egypt and used the same hieroglyphic script. Even their idols had the same facial expression.

When the body of Pharaoh Ramses was found, doctors observed traces of nicotine in his body. This indicates that Ramses had access to tobacco. Since it has been determined that tobacco originated in pre-Columbian America, it means the Phoenicians who were the tradesmen of Egypt, were trading with the people of America dating back before the Christian era.

The people of Tyre were master Seamen. They traveled the world in their ships and carried on trade with all the peoples of the world. They were known and feared by the brothers in Africa along with their enemies in the Caucasoid Mountains of Europe.

When Europe was inhabited by barbaric tribes and roamed by half-dressed white men, the Black inhabitants of Tyre, later to be called Phoenicians, put fear into the hearts of all maritime nations with their ships that traveled as fast as the wind.

The Phoenicians always lived on the coast and the world was their trading partner. These Black men came and went bringing with them the greatest of the world's goods.

The Historian Josephus writes

# TYRIAN OR PHOENICIAN CITIZENS OF ZION

*"Now the children of Ham possessed the land from Syria and Amanus, and the mountains of Libanus, seizing upon all that was on its sea coast and as far as the ocean and keeping it as their own..*[30]

Many are still wondering how the Phoenicians accomplished the task of building an empire. They were such a tiny people, yet were able to develop storehouses and hideaways that had more bounty than many kings could acquire in their lifetime. Even their powerful Black brothers who ruled Egypt and Babylonia could only dream of achieving some of the feat of the Phoenicians.

Tyre was one of the strongest and most beautiful cities of the ancient world. Hiram, in 1000 BC, constructed his palace on the sea and they called the town Zor, which means rock. It boasted one of the greatest and safest harbors in the world and was home of the tallest and most handsome men who ever lived, rivaled only by the Ethiopians of Africa, according to the Greek Historians.

The Tyrians were shrewd and skillful merchants who by 600 BC had built trading posts all over the world. One author writes:

*"On the Bosphorus, in Italy, Sicily, on the Spanish and African coasts. They developed trading posts in Thasos Cythera, Thera, Crete Melos and all Greek cities"*[31]

All over the countries of the Mediterranean one could find their vessels. They carried flasks, glass beads and glazed tiles. There is no doubt that these Black men, were the first mass producers of consumer goods.

---

[30] Josephus, Flavious. *Antiquities of the Jews* (London: Printed for J. Cooke, No. 17, Pater-noster-Row, [1785-1786]), 31.
[31] Herm, Gerhard "*The Phoenicians*, (New York: Williams Morrow and Company Inc. 1975), 21.

Black Citizens of Zion

Herodotus describes how the Phoenicians would go to a beach, spread out their goods on the shores, then return to their ships and set a fire. The people of the town seeing the fire would then journey to the site of the goods and there place their gold or silver. The Phoenicians would then return to check the sum of gold. If it was not enough to cover the cost of the goods, they would return to their ships and wait. The buyers would keep adding gold until all were satisfied, them the goods would be touched and the gold would be taken.

The Phoenicians were not always honest in their dealings with everyone as can be ascertained from the following passage.

> *"As they traveled the world, they discovered new goods and services. They found in Spain the rich silver mines of the Sierra Morena which were worked by the indigenous Iberians. Diodorus Siculus, a rather superficial Greek Historiographer, relates that these men were so ignorant, that they did not know what to do with the precious metal until the Phoenicians on their trading voyages offered them small amounts of their goods for the silver."* [32]

The Phoenicians are believed to have visited America and many other places in the early AD's, but many American scholars are afraid to investigate the facts. It appears that the last thing certain scholars would like to admit, is that a Black nation crossed the Atlantic Ocean and discovered America, long before any white man had learned how to handle a ship properly. Ivan Van Sertima in his book "They came before Columbus," argues that coins from Cyrene and Carthage were discovered in America in an American village along with hundreds of inscription of the Phoenician alphabet. He also asserts that Phoenicians artifacts were found in Pennsylvania and New York, yet American scientists and geologist have refused to look at the inscriptions because they refuse to acknowledge the Phoenicians came here before Columbus.

---

[32] Ibid 137.

# TYRIAN OR PHOENICIAN CITIZENS OF ZION

It is interesting to note that in the white societies, the Phoenicians developed separate communities and trading post. While in Africa they found lodgings in ordinary housings, developing in Memphis a district called the Tyrian quarters.

> *"Thus in 600 BC the Phoenicians build a trading station on Ibiza; a little earlier they were already installed in Malta and the neighboring Island of Goxo. We know that there were at least three Phoenician settlements in Sicily, at Motya, Panormus and Soloeis, all on the northern tip of the island."*[33]

> *"In 1972 Phoenicians graves of the seventh Century BC were also discovered near Mozia, on the west coast of Sicily, in accordance with Thucydides account stating that he Tyrians had more or less had the whole island in their power....Now archeologists backs this up."*[34]

> *"They circled the continent of Africa before the Portuguese, a feat so impressive that when the Portuguese achieved it some years after they were regarded as the greatest sailors ever."*[35]

> *"Their agents stood as counselors behind the thrones of Egypt, whispered advice into the ears of Assyrian, Babylonian and Persian Kings....Wherever one went it seemed impossible to shake them"*[36]

They were ingenious traders and topnotch engineers. They had very little to trade, but made the most of what they had, building it out to the natural resources they found around them.

---

[33] Ibid
[34] Ibid 138.
[35] Herm, Gerhard *The Phoenicians*, (New York, Williams Morrow and Company Inc. 1975), 141.
[36] Herm, Gerhard *The Phoenicians*, (New York, Williams Morrow and Company Inc. 1975), 14.

## Black Citizens of Zion

One of their greatest achievements was sand. They realized it contained quartz and they were able to develop the making of glass, a secret many believe they stole from their brothers in Egypt. They also managed to use the small warm-water snail found on their beaches to produce purple dye, for which they became famous.

The nation of Tyre, because it was built on a rock in the ocean, had no springs and the people could not dig wells. They were totally dependent on rain water which was probably undrinkable during the long summers. According to the Historian Strabo they captured springs that gushed out of the sea bed. From their boats they laid down turned funnel over the freshwater sources in the salt water so that the waters were driven upwards by its own pressure and could be caught.

The Phoenicians mastered the art of shipbuilding, sailing and the development of Astronomy. With the help of Pharaoh and their Black brothers in Egypt, they even built the first Suez Canal.

When David decided to build the temple of Yahweh, it was to the Phoenicians that he turned. The Phoenicians supplied the lumber, workmen and all the expertise that was needed for the finishing of this magnificent structure. Solomon, David's Black son, was later to invest jointly with the Phoenicians in silver mining, a venture some prophets of Israel resented; due to the fact the Phoenicians would at times encourage the breaking of the Sabbath for the purpose of financial gain. This would later lead to the punishment of the Phoenicians by God himself.

According to the Old Testament book of Ezekiel, no one could sing like the sons of Tyre. Traders in purple and gold, they were epiphany of GQ himself, sharpest dresser of their time, and obsessed with their beauty and riches.

> *" 28:2 Son of man, say unto the prince of Tyre, Thus saith the Lord GOD; Because thine heart is lifted up, and thou hast said, I am a God, I sit in the seat of*

# TYRIAN OR PHOENICIAN CITIZENS OF ZION

> *God, in the midst of the seas; yet thou art a man, and not God, though thou set thine heart as the heart of God: 28:3 Behold, thou art wiser than Daniel; there is no secret that they can hide from thee: 28:4 With thy wisdom and with thine understanding thou hast gotten thee riches, and hast gotten gold and silver into thy treasures: 28:5 By thy great wisdom and by thy traffic hast thou increased thy riches, and thine heart is lifted up because of thy riches."(Ezekiel 28:2-5)*

Phoenicia started as a free and independent nation. Like all the nations of Palestine however, Phoenicia became subject to the various other powers that ruled this area of the world. The most powerful of the neighbors of Phoenicia was Egypt, one of the first major empires. This African nation seems to have exerted a powerful influence over Phoenicia until the coming of the Hittites. Thutmose III Pharaoh of Egypt writes

> *"Every year real cedars of Lebanon are fell for me and brought to my court... When my army returns, they bring as tribute the cedars of my victory, which I have won according to the designs of my father, who has entrusted all foreign lands to me. I have left none for the Asiatic,"*[37]

According to the Grolier Electronic Encyclopedia, Phoenicia becomes a dominant world power free of Egypt with the coming of the Hittites. The Egyptian kings were too taken up with their own problems to protect their vassal states, so the land of Phoenicia was born. This was sealed when Ramses II and Khkattushilish III signed a treaty and Ramses accepts Khkattushilish III daughter for a wife. From now on Canaan is Phoenicia.

When Assyria was the dominant power the Phoenicians did not accept it as calmly as they did Egyptian ruler-ship. They

---

[37] Herm, Gerhard *The Phoenicians*, (New York: Williams Morrow and Company Inc. 1975), 148.

## Black Citizens of Zion

appeared to have resented Asian rule. The constant fighting weakened the Phoenicians however, and they regained their strength only when the Black brothers of Babylonia defeated the Assyrians and destroyed Nineveh in 612 BC. Phoenicia again became a dominant nation.

Nebuchadnezzar, king of Babylon, tried with his massive well-trained army to take Tyre, but could not take the city. The Phoenicians were smart and mysterious and "wiser than the biblical prophet Daniel" so eventually Nebuchadnezzar abandoned his task.

> *"Nebuchadnezzar tried to take Tyre." For thirteen years, from 585 to 572 BC, the largest army of the day lay before a tiny Island fortress and was unable to take it."* [38]
>
> *The Tyrians, getting their supplies by sea, countered each assault, defeated every attempt to build a dam and bore with incredible staunchness the inevitable hardship of the siege."* [39]

With the downfall of the Babylonian Empire came Cyrus II and the Persians. The Persians were badly in need of the ships of the Phoenicians to control the Mediterranean basin and conquer Egypt. This task was impossible without the aid of the Phoenicians. A treaty was signed with the Phoenicians that made them Persia's allies. Cambyses then attacked Egypt in 525 BC with Phoenicia as a reluctant partner. The men of Tyre were uneasy about attacking their Black brothers in Egypt. Cambyses' next move was an attack on Carthage. This idea was abandoned when the Tyrians made it clear they would not attack their brothers in the Phoenician city of Carthage.

With the fall of Persia came a new power, Hellenism. As the Persians battled the Greeks who were rebelling against their rule, it was the Phoenicians who paved the way for the fighting

---

[38] Arrian "The Campaigns of Alexander" (London: Penguin Books. October 1976), 158.
[39] Ibid 153.

## TYRIAN OR PHOENICIAN CITIZENS OF ZION

at Sea. They were the only sailors capable of defeating the Greeks who themselves, according to Josephus, had Black roots and seemed to have inherited the ability to be master seamen.

The Phoenicians were the stars at sea. This resulted in the Greeks hating the Phoenicians. The men of Greece made a decisive effort to destroy all record of Phoenicia. The rumor was also spread that the Phoenicians were a greedy people who sold out their brothers to the Persians. Eventually after Tyre was destroyed by Alexander the Great, Carthage the new stronghold of the Phoenicians was hated by both Romans and Greeks.

In attempting to conquer the world, Alexander on His way to Egypt, must pass the Phoenician cities of Aradus, Byblos, Berytus, Sidon and Tyre. At Tyre he requested co-operation with his army receiving acceptance from every city but Tyre. Tyre rejected his request thinking he was no threat to their invincible navy and well-fortified city. They were also not sure who would eventually become the dominant world power, Alexander or Darius.

Alexander then met with His army to apprise them of the situation, these were his words.

> *"Friends and fellow soldiers, I do not see how we can safely advance upon Egypt, so long as Persia controls the sea; and to pursue Darius with the neutral city of Tyre in our rear and Egypt and Cyprus still in enemy hands would be a serious risk, especially in view of the situation in Greece. With our army on the track of Darius, far inland in the direction of Babylon, the Persians might well regain control of the coast, and thus be enabled with more power behind them to transfer the war to Greece, where Sparta is already openly hostile to us, and at the moment but a unwilling ally; fear, not friendliness keeping her on our side. But with Tyre destroyed, all Phoenicia would be ours, and the*

*Phoenician fleet, which both in numbers and quality is the predominant element in the sea power of Persia, would very likely come over to us. The Phoenician seamen, ships crews or fighting men, once their towns are in our hands, will hardly endure to face the perils of service at sea for the sake of others. ...And with the united fleets of Macedonia and Phoenicia, our supremacy at sea would be guaranteed, and the expedition to Egypt would thus be a simple matter, and finally with Egypt in our hands we shall have no further cause for uneasiness about Greece. We shall be able to march on Babylon with security at home, with enhanced prestige, and with Persia excluded not only from the sea, but from the whole continent up to the Euphrates."*[40]

Alexander had a tremendous task. Great armies had tried it before him and failed. The Tyrian fleet was strong and unbeatable at sea, especially with Persia still in the picture. Furthermore the island was surrounded by strong and lofty walls.

The plan was laid to construct a path across the water to the city with the many rocks which were lying around. This they hoped would allow the heavy machinery to be brought close to the city walls in an attempt to create a breach.

When the work began, Alexander walked and inspected the work himself, giving praises to his men and special reward for good work.

Before long the ramp came within the range of the missiles from the city, and the Tyrians made constant raids on various points along the path making the work impossible. The Macedonians then mounted their heavy artillery equipment on the ramp built thus far in an attempt to protect the workers and continue the work as best they could.

---

[40]Ibid 161.

## TYRIAN OR PHOENICIAN CITIZENS OF ZION

The Tyrians responded by setting a ship on fire and sailing it into the ramp. When the ramp began to burn they came out and set fire to every piece of machinery. This made Alexander furious, and more determined than ever to take the city.

Alexander ordered the work resumed and made the ramp much wider to give more artillery support. The engineers were ordered to construct fresh engines while one General journeyed to Sidon to muster as many ships as could be found. It had dawn upon the Macedonians that without the help of the other Phoenician cities, they were no match for the tiny city of Tyre.

Alexander was lucky to gather a multitude of Vessels from Cyprus, Soli, Sidon, Aradus and Byblos who decided to side with Alexander realizing that Darius had lost at Issus.

With the coming of the ships, the Tyrians threw blocks of stones into the harbor so the ships find no safe passage to the city. When a ship did make it through the dangerous path, the Tyrians responded with an array of fire making all the ship captains opposed to attacking the city by sea for fear of the destruction of their vessels.

As Alexander's men tried to finish the ramp, the Tyrians kept attacking and destroying ships. Alexander soon blockaded the harbor with his ships to keep them from attacking his ramp, but the Tyrians sent divers out to cut the ship's anchors. The Macedonians then used chains to moor their ships and proceeded to remove the many stones cast into the harbor by the Tyrians. The Tyrians then attacked and destroyed many of the squadrons including those which were blockading their city. The remaining squadrons which were not destroyed were driven ashore. This infuriated Alexander and made him more determined to capture this Black city.

After many months, the ramp was finally completed and the bombardment of the city began. Alexander took one garrison and attacked the city from one direction while the men on the ramp did the same. A breach was finally made and ship loads

## Black Citizens of Zion

of men were brought in with backup fire to protect them. Alexander himself led the way through the breach, and fierce fighting ensued. Note the following words:

> *"The Tyrians made Alexander pay for every square foot of ground with streams of blood, but the King's punch paid off. Away from the water his opponents were like birds with their wings torn off, or magicians bereft of their magic hats. Now they had only the ordinary strength of ordinary men, and it was not enough"*[41]

> *"Alexander was not only taking a town, but he was also destroying a myth and must have been fully conscious of the fact....He made a hideous example of Tyre. Crosses were hewn for two thousand male citizens, and set up along the shores of the island. Thirty thousand women, children and older people were sold into slavery."*[42]

The slaughter was terrible. The Macedonians who had besieged the city for seven years acted as savages. 8,000 men were slaughtered and some 30,000 sold into slavery. It was the end of another great Black empire.

Alexander had one thing on his side, destiny. God had said he would eventually rule the world. Hundreds of years before his birth it was ordained that the Tyrians, because of their proud heart, would be destroyed, and another Black race would look on and realize the tragedy of not following Yahweh and would be sorrowful and repent. Had it not been for God's divine prediction, it might have been that Alexander would never have taken Tyre. Consider the following passage.

---

[41] Herm, Gerhard, *The Phoenicians*, (New York: Williams Morrow and Company Inc. 1975), 15.
[42] Ibid.

## TYRIAN OR PHOENICIAN CITIZENS OF ZION

> *"3 And Tyrus did build herself a stronghold, and heaped up silver as the dust, and fine gold as the mire of the streets. 4 Behold, the Lord will cast her out, and he will smite her power in the sea; and she shall be devoured with fire. 5 Ashkelon shall see it, and fear; Gaza also shall see it, and be very sorrowful, and Ekron; for her expectation shall be ashamed; and the king shall perish from Gaza, and Ashkelon shall not be inhabited."(Zechariah 9:3-6).*

Thus because of their proud and arrogant heart, God brought judgment upon the men of Tyre. According to the Sons of Korah however, when one gets to the city of Zion, the Tyrians will be represented there, "BLACK CITIZENS OF ZION"

Black Citizens of Zion

Philistine Warrior

# CHAPTER 6

## *PHILISTINE CITIZENS OF ZION*

*"10:6 And the sons of Ham; Cush, and Mizraim, and Phut, and Canaan.*
*10:13 And Mizraim begat Ludim, and Anamim, and Lehabim, and Naphtuhim,*
*10:14 And Pathrusim, and Casluhim, (out of whom came Philistine,) and Caphtorim." (Genesis 10:6, 13 & 14)*

According to the Bible, the Philistines were descendant of Captor, the seventh son of Mizraim. Mizraim was the Grandson of Ham, thus we can conclude that the Philistines were a Black race - or at least descendants of a Black race.

After God had confused the language of Nimrod and his people in order to prevent them from building a tower that stretched into the heaven, Captor and his family journeyed to the Island of Crete and settled there. In Crete, the Philistines built one of the earliest and greatest civilizations in the history of mankind. This civilization has come down in history as the Minoan civilization.[43]

The Philistines are popularized today in the so called Myth of the Island of Atlantis, an Island that is supposed to have disappeared under the sea. It is my contention that the disappearance of this Island was the reason for the Philistine's arrival in Palestine, and Greece. It was the Philistine who upgraded Greek Civilization by introducing the alphabet and

---
[43]Diop, Cheikh Anta, *Civilization or Barbarism* (NY: Lawrence Hill Books. 1991 Edition: 1st edition), 83.

Minoan art to these islands in 1420 BC. This of course is in direct contradiction to the conclusion of modern scholars who believe the destruction of Minoan or Philistine civilization was the result of an Achaean invasion.[44]

Atlantis disappeared due to a severe earthquake. This earthquake which many believe was the explosion of the Santorini Volcano. According to Egyptian documents the Santorini Volcano erupted during the XVIIIth Egyptian Dynasty and forced the descendants of Captor to migrate to Canaan. God later took responsibility for bringing the Philistine to Canaan in the Old Testament book of Amos 9:7.

> *" 9:7 Are ye not as children of the Ethiopians unto me, O children of Israel? saith the LORD. Have not I brought up Israel out of the land of Egypt? and the Philistines from Captor and the Syrians from Kir?"*

The Philistines or Minoans or Keftiu as they were called in the Egyptian documents, built a civilization of plowmen and fishermen. "They cultivated cereals, made flour, extracted olive oil, raised sheep and goats, made decorated vases, and were familiar with gold and probably copper."[45]

These Philistines or Minoan built a palace which was the exact replica of the Egyptians, and the very name Minos seems to be only a slight alteration of the name of the first semi-legendary Egyptian King; Menes.[46] This appears to indicate close ties between the Philistines and Egyptians, and that they were fully aware of the ties of brotherhood between themselves and the other Black races that lived on the continent of Africa.

Various Papyrus describing events in Egypt around the time of the eruption of the Santorini Volcano are now in our possession. Of course since the Bible describes the plagues of Egypt as happening round about this time, it is difficult to

---

[44] Ibid 72.
[45] Ibid 71.
[46] Ibid

## PHILISTINE CITIZENS OF ZION

differentiate whether these papyrus refer to the Volcanic eruption or the pestilence brought on by Moses, but either indicates beyond the question of a doubt, the accuracy of the Bible. Note the following:

> *"Trouble has beset the eyes. For nine days nobody had left the palace. There has been nine days of violence and tempest. Nobody, neither God nor man, is able to see his neighbor's face. We do not know what has happened throughout the Earth... It is a confusion that you brought upon the entire Earth with the sound of an uproar... Oh, let the Earth stop rumbling... Towns are destroyed... Upper Egypt is devastated... Blood is everywhere... Pestilence, looting are everywhere on the earth."[47]*

> *The sun is veiled and does not shine visibly in the eyes of men. No one can live when the sun is covered by clouds. God himself has abandoned men. If the sun shines, it is just for one hour. No one knows when it is noon; one cannot discern one's own shadow... He {Ra} is in the sky looking like the moon."[48]*

The same Papyrus also mentions the breaking of relationship between Egypt and Crete.

> *"The men will not sail toward Byblos today. What will we do to obtain cedar wood for our mummies and the burial of priests, and oil form faraway Crete to embalm the dignitaries? They {these Products} no longer come. What an important thing it is that the oasis people bring their spices during the feasts.[49]*

The nation of the Philistine is popular in the Bible as the home of Delilah. A woman of bewitching beauty who was responsible for the capture of the Hebrew Judge Samson. Obviously the beauty of these Black Philistine women was something that

---

[47] Ibid.
[48] Ibid 82
[49] Ibid.

## Black Citizens of Zion

captivated the Hebrew men, since they made it a habit to marry these women.  Samson himself appears to have been unable to live without one, even after his first marriage to a Philistine ended in disaster.  Sampson did not realize that in all races there are women, who will take your money, pluck your eyes out, and abandon you penniless and blind.  It was a lesson he learnt the hard way.

This nation was noted as a nation of Giants.  It was the home of Goliath and his brothers, men who like the Ethiopians and Phoenicians, stood head and shoulder above the crowd.  They were tremendous warriors who had mastered the use of weapons and chariots of iron.  This mastery which made them unbeatable even by the larger nations which existed around them.

Small but powerful, the Philistines constantly fought against the Hebrews.  At times they held the Hebrew tribes captives, while other times, they were held in submission.

The first time the Philistine appeared in scripture, they were regarded by God as a righteous people.  This is best emphasized in the story of their experience with Abraham recorded in the Old Testament book of Genesis.

> *"20:4 But Abimelech had not come near her: and he said, Lord, wilt thou slay also a righteous nation? GENESIS 20:5 Said he not unto me, She is my sister? and she, even she herself said, he is my brother: in the integrity of my heart and innocence of my hands have I done this." (Genesis 20:4)*

Abraham, the father of the Jews as he is called, traveled to the land of the Philistine to avoid a famine which had overtaken his home town.  Realizing his wife was very beautiful and might be desired by the men who lived in the city, Abraham laid down a plan to protect himself at the expense of his wife.  He arranged with his wife that they would tell the people of the city that they are brother and sister rather than risk death at the hands of the

# PHILISTINE CITIZENS OF ZION

Philistine. Abraham was not aware that the people of Philistine belonged to God. In typical religious arrogance, he probably thought he and his people were the only servants of the true God. He was not aware that these people respected and feared God, and that God had laid down a plan to protect the king from the lies of Abraham.

> *20:6 "And God said unto him in a dream, Yea, I know that thou didst this in the integrity of thy heart; for I also withheld thee from sinning against me: therefore suffered I thee not to touch her." (Genesis 20:6)*

This nation is believed to have been allied with the Phoenicians. They gave the land of Palestine its name, and spread over the whole district of Lebanon, the valley of Jordan, the island of Crete and many other Mediterranean islands.

According to the 9th chapter of the Old Testament Book of Zechariah, God had a special burden for the Black Races that lived in a Syria. This led to the destruction of Tyre, so the Philistines would see God's action and come to repentance. This was accomplished with the coming of Alexander the great, who was responsible for the destruction of the city of Tyre.

> *"3 And Tyrus did build herself a stronghold, and heaped up silver as the dust, and fine gold as the mire of the streets. 4 Behold, the Lord will cast her out, and he will smite her power in the sea; and she shall be devoured with fire. Ashkelon shall see it, and fear; Gaza also shall see it, and be very sorrowful, and Ekron; for her expectation shall be ashamed; and the king shall perish from Gaza, and Ashkelon shall not be inhabited." (Zechariah 9:3-6)*

The destruction of the Black Nation of Tyre was to lead to a fear of God among the cities of the Philistines. It would also somehow lead to the destruction of their king. The context appears to speak not just to the destruction of a local king, but

## Black Citizens of Zion

the destruction of their god king. God was about to establish a new world order in the cities of Philistia. This would lead to a new style of leadership. This new leadership was not what they had been exposed to previously; it was not in keeping with the old leadership but was a new brand of leadership. It was leadership that would be considered foreign. This leadership led to the abolition of sacrifices and abominations. More importantly, it caused the Philistines to become the people of Yahweh and assimilated into the Jewish nation. This was the experience of the Jebusites who were also assimilated into the Jewish nation. God would then give Philistia the same protection He gave Israel. The result would be the king of Israel riding into Jerusalem on a donkey. Consider the following passages taken from the Book of Zechariah 9:6-9, the Living Bible.

> *Zechariah 9:6 "And a bastard shall dwell in Ashdod and I will cut off the pride of the Philistines.*
> *Living Bible: I will yank her idolatry out of her mouth, and pull from her teeth her sacrifices that she eats with blood. Everyone left will worship God and be adopted into Israel as a new clan: the Philistines of Ekron will intermarry with the Jews, just as the Jebusites did so long ago. And I will surround my Temple like a guard to keep invading armies from entering Israel. I am closely watching their movements and I will keep them away; no foreign oppressors will again overrun my people's land."*
> *``Rejoice greatly, O my people! Shout with joy! For look—your king is coming! He is the Righteous One, the Victor! Yet he is lowly, riding on a donkey's colt!"*

God would put a bastard king upon the throne of Ashdod, which according to the division of the land among the tribes in the book of Joshua, was Judaic territory. This king shall be Philistine and Hebrew, Black and Jewish, Hametic and Shemite. This king would cause the abominations to cease, and all living in the territory would be considered God's people.

## PHILISTINE CITIZENS OF ZION

They would become leaders in Israel, just as the Black Jebusites were absorbed into the army of David when he overran the city of Jerusalem. God would then become the protector of this people who would be both Philistine and Jews. He will keep watch with His own eyes and no one would be able to over-run his people again. The king of Israel, whom the context suggests will be the bastard king of the Philistia, would go riding into Jerusalem as a king riding upon a mule. The intent of the passage therefore is to indicate that God would be the king of both Philistines and Jews. Furthermore He would be a bastard king, which means He would be conceived out of wedlock, or would be of mixed lineage, part Canaanite and part Jewish.

Of course, anyone who studies the lineage of Jesus will recognize that this was indeed true. It is interesting that the so-called curse of Canaan pronounced by a drunk who had just consumed too much wine, if it was eternally binding, would have passed on to Jesus, who was not just descendant of the Jews, but also of the various Canaanite and Hametic people who had married into His lineage. The following passages are worth considering.

> *"38:2 And Judah saw there a daughter of a certain Canaanite, whose name was Shuah; and he took her, and went in unto her." (Genesis 38:2)*

> *"2:1 And Joshua the son of Nun sent out of Shittim two men to spy secretly, saying, Go view the land, even Jericho. And they went, and came into an harlot's house, named Rahab, and lodged there. 17 And the city shall be accursed, even it, and all that are therein, to the LORD: only Rahab the harlot shall live, she and all that are with her in the house, because she hid the messengers that we sent." (Joshua 2:1 & 17)*

> *" 6:23 And the young men that were spies went in, and brought Rahab, and her father, and her mother, and*

*her brethren, and all that she had; and they brought out all her kindred, and left them without the camp of Israel.....:25 And Joshua saved Rahab the harlot alive, and her father's household, and all that she had; and she dwelleth in Israel even unto this day; because she hid the messengers, which Joshua sent to spy out Jericho."(Joshua 6:23 & 25)*

*MAT 1:5 "And Salmon begat Boaz of Rachab; and Boaz begat Obed of Ruth; and Obed begat Jesse;"*

*2 Samuel 11:3 "And David sent and inquired after the woman. And one said, Is not this Bath-Sheba, the daughter of Eliam, the wife of Uriah the Hittite?"*

*2 SAMUEL 12:24 "And David comforted Bath-Sheba his wife, and went in unto her, and lay with her: and she bare a son, and he called his name Solomon: and the LORD loved him."*

It appears that the predominant non-Jewish link of the descendants of Jesus was indeed Canaanite. Recognizing also that the Children of Israel and particularly the Tribes of Judah and Benjamin co-habituated with the Canaanites, Jebusites, Hittites and other Black races that settled Palestine, it might very well be that by the time of Jesus, one had difficulty differentiating between Jews and Ethiopians as is stated by certain historians.

*Ezra 9:2" For they have taken of their daughters for themselves, and for their sons: so that the holy seed have mingled themselves with the people of those lands: yea, the hand of the princes and rulers hath been chief in this trespass."*

*Judges 1:27-33 "27 Neither did Manasseh drive out the inhabitants of Bethshean and her towns, nor Taanach and her towns, nor the inhabitants of Dor and her towns, nor the inhabitants of Ibleam and her towns, nor the inhabitants of Megiddo and her towns: but the Canaanites would dwell in that land. 28 And it came to pass, when Israel was strong, that they put the Canaanites to tribute, and did not utterly drive them out. 29 Neither did Ephraim drive out the Canaanites that dwelt in Gezer; but the Canaanites dwelt in Gezer among them. 30 Neither did Zebulun drive out the inhabitants of Kitron, nor the inhabitants of Nahalol; but the Canaanites dwelt among them, and became tributaries. 31 Neither did Asher drive out the inhabitants of Accho, nor the inhabitants of Zidon, nor of Ahlab, nor of Achzib, nor of Helbah, nor of Aphik, nor of Rehob: 32 But the Asherites dwelt among the Canaanites, the inhabitants of the land: for they did not drive them out. 33 Neither did Naphtali drive out the inhabitants of Beth-she'mesh, nor the inhabitants of Bethanath; but he dwelt among the Canaanites, the inhabitants of the land: nevertheless the inhabitants of Beth-she'mesh and of Bethanath became tributaries unto them"*

I think the Black race should take special pride in Jesus the Savior of the world. He is our own. This is not just because He is God of all the people, which He is, but he has the blood of the descendants of Ham flowing through His veins. In fact, He probably was the color of Ham himself. According to the Sons of Korah, when we get to heaven, the Nation of Philistine will be represented there among the "BLACK CITIZENS OF ZION".

# Black Citizens of Zion

88

# CHAPTER 7

## ETHIOPIAN CITIZENS OF ZION

*Genesis 10:6 "and the sons of Ham; Cush, and Mizraim, and Phut, and Canaan."*

Ethiopia in the Bible is called "the land of Cush". It consisted of the continent of Africa below Egypt, a continent stretching for some 12 million square miles, 22 % of the world's land-mass and only 16% of the world's population.

Ethiopia is a land of fascinating contrast, dense tropical forest, vast stretches of savanna land, mountains, lakes, rivers, arid desert and even snow at the top of Mount Kilimanjaro.

Most Scholars believe the land of Cush or Africa as it is called today was the home of the Garden of Eden. The oldest bones discovered were found in this region of the world. Africa is regarded as the Mother of Civilizations, and the origin of all races, not just of Blacks, as the word Ethiopia suggests.

Jesus lived on the continent of Africa during the early years of His life. When he chooses His disciples, some argue that at least one of them was a Black man. One must admit however, that it is very likely that all the disciples were Black since Israel had intermarried extensively with the indigenous Black population. We do know that by the time Jesus died on the cross, many Africans had become believers. The Ethiopian Eunuch, Simon of Cyrene, Rufus, Simon the Black disciple of Jesus also called Niger, Paul of Tarsus along with the multitudes who were converted on the day of Pentecost must have returned to their homeland to spread the Gospel of Jesus Christ.

It was in Africa that the strongest churches were to develop, which challenged the very authority of Rome itself. The African church was so strong, with its center at Alexandria in Egypt that ultimately there was a split between the African church and the Roman church,

Africa flourished as a Christian Center, and even though the first leader of an African nation to be won to Christ according to recorded history took place in the fourth century with the conversion of Ezna, the king of Ethiopia, the people of Africa had been Christian for centuries before and were in close contact with their Lord and Master

When the world itself followed after Catholicism, and the Crusades and Holy wars raged, there was one nation quietly serving God in seclusion. Cut off by Moslems invaders, and fighting for survival, the "Land of the Cushites" vigilantly upheld the gospel of Jesus Christ. During the centuries when the church was to turn form the true Sabbath to Sunday-keeping, the Ethiopians or Cushites as they called themselves, committed their ways to God, and upheld the name of His Son and His Sabbath. Here sprang up a true breed of Christianity preached by Christ in the first century. It was a Christianity deeply rooted in the African soil, with no taint of colonialism or Catholicism. The Africans worshipped God as Black men should worship God, with a lively service of praise and fervor.

The demise of Africa as a center of greatness Black pride and Christianity came with the coming of Islam. Mohammed, born in Mecca 570 AD, served at first to antagonize most of his fellow townsmen, and in 622 he was forced to flee for safety to Medina. A few years later the prophet returned with an army, cleansed the Kaaba of its idols and vigorously spread the tenets of his faith throughout Arabia. After Mohammed's death in 632 AD his monotheistic teachings were compiled in what became known as the Koran, the Holy of the Holiest to all Muslims and the repository of Islamic doctrine and obligations.

# ETHIOPIAN CITIZENS OF ZION

> *"Then followed on of the most amazing epoch of religious expansion in history. Mohammed had succeeded in organizing the Arabs into a militant proselytizing force which set about to annex new territories and peoples under the banner of Islam. Within some forty years they had conquered territory extending from Tunisia through Egypt and across the Fertile Crescent to include Iraq and Persia. Within a century of the Prophet's death, Muslims had stormed into the Iberian Peninsula and over the Pyrenees to be turned back only after reaching Tours in central France."*[50]

Islam now compassed three continents and the sale of African slaves followed the goods that crossed the continents. The Africans were told to convert, or be enslaved. Many chose slavery because they were Christians, and Christians they would die.

> *"From the earliest times, the elimination of African states as independent African sovereignties had been an Asian objective"*[51]

They came as trading partners and were allowed to set up their trading posts. They hired Black soldiers to protect their goods, and then used the army against its people. Africa was a Christian community, and the Moslems would not have this so close to the center of Islam which was just across the Red Sea.

Islam would have us believe that the Muslim faith is the natural religion of the sons of Ham. This is far from the truth. Consider the following facts:

---

[50] Carroll, Harry J., ed. *The development of Civilization; a documentary history of politics, society and thoughts.* Glenview, Ill.}Scott, Foresman [1969]) 154.

[51] Williams, Chancellor *The Destruction of Black Civilization* (Chicago Illinois: Third World Press, 1976), 50.

1.     Rome accepted Christianity in 322 AD with the conversion of Constantine.

2.     Christianity entered England in 597.

3.     It came to Germany in 476 when Rome fell to the Barbarians and to Russia in 956 when Vladimir the grand Prince of Kiev accepted Christ as his savior.

4.     On the other hand, Philip talked to the Ethiopian Eunuch in AD 30-40 when he was sent by Amanateree Queen of Ethiopia to bring back the truth concerning Jesus of Nazareth.

5.     Simon of Cyrene was in Jerusalem at the crucifixion in AD 31 and was responsible for helping Jesus carry the cross to Golgotha.

This suggest that Christianity is the black man's natural religion, not Islam, not Rastafarianism, not Catholicism,

Africa is a land whose people knew not the meaning of failure. Whenever adversities came and powerful armies were introduce, unlike any other nation on earth, the African showed a remarkable ability to pick up the pieces of their lives, and start another great kingdom in some other location.

When United Egypt fell, Nubia, then Meroe, became the center of Black power. Then there was Ethiopia or Axum center of Christianity. This nation's territory was called the Land of the God's, where Christian churches flourished in magnificence and beauty. It was from this land that the Queen of Sheba left her Nubian home and traveled to Israel to see if all the things she had heard about the Black king Solomon was true. Up until them Ethiopia, which ruled Egypt, was the dominant Black nation, and the thought of a king wiser that the Pharaoh of Egypt was ridiculous, especially from a people recently enslaved by Egypt.

History has it that when the Nubian queen came to Solomon, they conceived a son called Menelek. He became a famous

# ETHIOPIAN CITIZENS OF ZION

Ethiopian ruler and his lineage ruled Ethiopia for some 2000 years.

It was Cyriacus king of Kings as he was called in Africa that marched against Islamic ruled Egypt with 100,000 soldiers and commanded the Muslims to refrain from destroying churches and persecuting Christians or feel the might of African soldiers. Egypt quickly agreed, and the African army soon withdrew.

Then there was Ghana, traders of the world. Their land was a thriving economy of gold, ivory, paper, copper, emerald, ebony and ostridge feathers. A strong economy meant a strong army. One that was feared by both Egypt and the armies of the world. The men of Ghana were militant Africans. They resisted amalgamation with the whites and Asiatic, unlike the Africans of Egypt. To the people of Ghana, the rejection of their culture was an insult to their ancestors and their God.

Songhi was an African kingdom that specialized in scholarship. In Songhi it is reported that people made more money selling books than gold. It was in Songhi that the famous University of Timbuktu was organized. This university boasted the greatest library in the world. Men came for Greece, Europe, Arabia, Spain and Palestine to study at the feet of the great African scholars.

Mali under the great king Mansa Musa built in 1312 AD one of the greatest empires of the fourteenth century.

Then there was Alwa. This was an African city with wide streets lined with palm tree, spacious homes, thriving industries and a strong army augmented by a strong cavalry.

Next was Funji. The people of Funji struggled to take back all Black land from both the Muslims and the Ottoman Turks who were laying claim to African soil.

Africa was the land which had what all people wanted most - Gold, diamonds, ivory, copper, iron ore, and a group of people that appeared to be physically superior in strength and intellect. It is the richest continent on earth, and it's remarkable that it has been the home of Black men and women for over 8,000 years.

According to Chancellor Williams, the Blacks of Africa were people excelling as a line of builders of empires dating back to the Stone Age. They had scholars, scientists, scribes architects, priests, mathematicians, engineers, and stone brick masons, and generals, carpenters, artists, sculptors, cloth makers, farmers, teachers, smiths and Blacksmiths.

Africa indeed was the cradle of civilization. This is so forcibly impressed upon history that the white man's answer was to make men's forefather a monkey and the African the first man from whom the white man later evolved.

> *"This continent was so rich, that according to Herodotus, the Africans bound their prisoners in golden chains in about 430 BC."*[52]

What happened to these great empire builders, the tall strong Black men, those geniuses who were the world's greatest businessmen? What changed for the brothers who sailed the seven seas in their ships that traveled faster than the wind? What happened to builders of civilization who gave mankind their first alphabet, the art of astronomy and medicine, its first democratic system and representative government? What happened that caused the Africans to be enslaved, their land divided, and Islamized, so that today people are starving on the richest continent on earth?

In times past, when war was coming, it was to Africa that men looked for military assistance. It was the men of Africa that had the might and ability to defeat the coming armies. When Senecharib was at the gates of Jerusalem and commanded Hezekiah to surrender the city, it was to Africa that word was

---

[52]Houston, Drusilla. *Wonderful Ethiopians of the ancient Cushite Empire*, Oklahoma City, Oklahoma: The Universal publishing co. 1926) 41.

## ETHIOPIAN CITIZENS OF ZION

sent, "come quickly, deliver your brothers from the hand of the king of Assyria", and Shitbitku ruler of Nubia, sent his brother Tarhaka to the assistance of the Black king Hezekiah, ruler of Israel.

When Senecharib was at the gates of Egypt the Egyptian king wrote to Ethiopia, "Let there be peace among us, let us come to a mutual understanding, let us divide the land between us, no foreigners should rule over us."

The Bible talks about Tarhaka and according to the Historian Strabo, Tarhaka conquered all lands as far as Europe. This African loved military power freedom and justice, these were their watchwords.

The Persian king Cambyses, after he had captured the Black Empire of Babylon because the Negro Nabonidus was a drunkard and too busy partying to protect his people and his city, decided Africa was ripe for the taking. The Black people of Africa posed a serious threat to his power base. Cambyses then sent spies into Africa and before long they were discovered. The king then demanded of them their reason for being in the motherland. The spies revealed to the king their mission and he reacted swiftly and wisely. Taking his massive bow in his hand and pulling as hard as he could, the King of Ethiopia fired the arrow. The instrument of war whisked through the leaves and found its mark in a distant tree. "Go tell your king, the Ethiopian said, "Go tell your king that until he can draw a bow as large, and fire it as far as the African, then he dare not enter Ethiopia, and until them, he should thank the God's who have not put it in the minds of the Sons of Ethiopia to win another man's country." Cambyses was so furious when he received the message, that he started to make immediate preparation to attack Ethiopia.

Thus from the beginning Africans were regarded as superior fighting men. People were beginning to trust the Black men, rather than God. God brought down the Black nations, because they were beginning to look to their own power, rather than to His. Note the following Old Testament passage.

> *ISAIAH 43:3 "For I am the LORD thy God, the Holy One of Israel, thy Saviour: I gave Egypt for thy ransom, Ethiopia and Seba for thee."*[53]

Thus God gave Egypt, Ethiopia and Seba for Israel. He caused the downfall of Africa to prove a point. The point was, whether Black or white, there was no race on earth powerful enough to withstand Him. He was the God who created and protected man. Even though the Africans had extraordinary strength and intellectual genius, should the African not turn to Him, he would bring his downfall. This was not just for the African, but any people who would not obey Him. Note the words of the Prophet Ezekiel:

> *EZEKIEL 30:4 "And the sword shall come upon Egypt, and great pain shall be in Ethiopia, when the slain shall fall in Egypt, and they shall take away her multitude, and her foundations shall be broken down. 5 Ethiopia, and Libya, and Lydia, and all the mingled people, and Chub, and the men of the land that is in league, shall fall with them by the sword." (Isaiah 43:3)*

It is clear to me that the time has come for the Cushites to return to God. In America we live in a land that has robbed us of our heritage. Our historical path we can trace no further back than slavery. They traveled in their ships and stole us from our homeland. Our Muslim brother encouraged it by selling our fore parents because they were Christians and resented Islam. Our kingly past, our royal heritage, our mighty forefathers have been robbed from our lineage and now we travel as a people without a history. God says however:

> *"11 And it shall come to pass in that day, that the Lord shall set his hand again the second time to*

# ETHIOPIAN CITIZENS OF ZION

*recover the remnant of his people, which shall be left,...from Egypt, and from Cush,...and from the islands of the sea."(Isaiah 11:11)*

Clearly Africans will gather from Egypt, Africa and the Islands of the sea. This should be good news for all of us. People of African descent everywhere should be excited that such a day is coming when Jesus will be in charge. A day when Black and whites the world over will give their hearts to God and racism will be no more. There will be no need for affirmative action on that day. "Men will be judged by the content of their character and not the color of their skins. It will be a day when Black men and white men will be able to join hands and sing in the words of the old Negro spiritual, free at last, free at last, thank God almighty I am free at last." When that day arrives, according to the Bible, something special will happen.

*"SPA 68:31 Princes shall come out of Egypt; Ethiopia shall soon stretch out her hands unto God." (Psalm 68:31)*

This is a message that God's people should be spreading all around the world to our Black brothers and sisters. We need to tell it on the mountains of Africa and in the suburbs of New York City. It should spread to the hills of Jamaica and in the ghettos of the Third World. Let it resound in the in the mosque of Allah and the kingdom Hall of the Jehovah Witnesses. Black men and women everywhere needs to know that out of Africa will come princes. This is not because blacks are born in the royal lineage of the Pharaohs, which we are. It is not because we are of a long line of Nubian Kings, which we are. It is because we are brothers of Jesus Christ, sons of God, and if I read my Bible correctly, this God is the Africans God, the Africans God forever, and through Him we are princes. Neither the Europeans nor Islam can deny us that privilege. God has made a promise to all that he will return again and received us unto ourselves. This promise reads:

*"1 Let not your heart be troubled: ye believe in God, believe also in me. 2 In my Father's house are many mansions: if it were not so, I would have told you. I go to prepare a place for you. 3 And if I go and prepare a place for you, I will come again, and receive you unto myself; that where I am, there ye may be also." (John 14:1-3)*

Our forefathers were enslaved for a long time. We have been taught that being Black means being second class citizens of the developed World. Third world nations indicate just that, third class status. Africa was divided by Europeans into 53 nations, running across tribal borders, family territories and language groups that have resulted in constant warfare so that Africa can never achieve its full potential. It was George Washington during the American Civil war who said, "Mississippi was meant to be the river of one nation." He knew America could not be great if she was divided, and men fought and died to keep this nation as one.

I believe the Nile too was meant to be the river of one nation. Africa was a great continent, but today it is divided into 53 nations. Its people are starving because Muslims are fighting Christians, and tribes are fighting tribes. They are cutting off each other from the sources of food and supplies. The times has come for Blacks to band together and tell the world God is gathering His remnant from Africa and the world, so you and I could be numbered among, "THE BLACK CITIZENS OF ZION."

# CHAPTER 8

## *LORD OF ZION*

*Psalm 87:6 "The LORD shall count, when he writeth up the people, that this man was born there."*

All the nations represented, Egypt, Philistia, Phoenicia, Babylon and Ethiopia were great Black nations. They made remarkable impact upon history. All had significant input and are revered by historians today. When one enters Zion, however, it is not the ancestral heritage that recommends them; it is the Lord of Zion who counts them as His own. It is therefore important to consider who is this Lord of Zion? Or who shall be the Lord of Zion?

In the black community today, many believe that Islam or Christianity has the answer to this question. Because of this, we will take a look at the central figures in these religions.

## MOHAMMED CE 570-632

On a strip called the Island of the Arabs 80 % of which is occupied by the country of Saudi Arabia, Mohammed, prophet of Islam was born in 570 AD in the city of Mecca. At the time of his birth, some 500 years after the death of Jesus, Africa was a Christian continent. The Abyssinians of Ethiopia were the major exporter of Christianity to Arabia and the Middle East. When the Jews or Arabs were mistreating Christians, it was the Africans who came to their rescue. The African church, known as the Coptic or Black Church had one of the earliest Bibles, now known as the Coptic Bible. This Bible is the largest Bible in the world, and includes the so-called Apocryphal books.

About 610 AD Mohammed received the first of a series of revelations that convinced him he was chosen as God's messenger. He began to preach the message entrusted to him—that there is but one God, to whom all humankind must commit themselves.

According to the Muslims, during the month Ramadan, or the month of April on our calendar, God transmitted the Koran to Mohammed, which after his death was compiled and written some thirty years later in four different versions by the warring factions who fought over the inheritance he left behind.

Mohammed tried to evangelize his people but was banished because of his theology. He returned in 632 with an army however, and a motto: "fight, until all men acknowledge there is no God but Allah."

Mecca was eventually conquered and dedicated to the worship of Allah. By the time of his death in 632, Mohammed had managed to organize the Arab tribe's people into a military proselytizing force that would storm the world.

The movement sent its armies across the entire Middle East, taking in its course, North Africa, Carthage, Palestine, Spain, and the Mediterranean cost. Today, Islam is the dominant religion in every country of Palestine except Israel.

Islam has four infallible source of teachings the most popular being the Koran. Muslims acknowledge this book as the actual words of God revealed to the Prophet Mohammed

The Koran asserts that its message is neither human invention nor innovation. Muslims claims it confirms and clarifies the scripture that Jews and Christians received earlier. It is interesting however that both Jewish and Old Testament scripture condemns books such as the Koran which seeks to get its authority from both these sacred books. Consider the passage from the Book of Revelation 22:18-19.

# LORD OF ZION

> *"For I testify unto every man that heareth the words of the prophecy of this book, If any man shall add unto these things, God shall add unto him the plagues that are written in this book: [19]And if any man shall take away from the words of the book of this prophecy, God shall take away his part out of the book of life, and out of the holy city, and from the things which are written in this book."*

According to the Christian scripture, if anyone adds or take away from the Bible, God will take his name from the book of life. Now surely anyone who reads the Koran would have to admit that it both add and detracts from the Christian scripture. This is true because the Koran is distinctly different and disagrees with most of the basic teaching of the Holy Bible. Consider the following Old Testament words:

> *Isaiah 8:20 "to the law and to the testimony: if they speak not according to this word, it is because there is no light in them."*

This again would disqualify the Koran form being inspired scripture. The Koran does not agree with the law and testimonies of the Hebrew scripture. Furthermore, the Old Testament scripture is built around the fact that God created a perfect man who sinned and needed redemption. God therefore formulated a plan to reconcile man to Himself. The plan necessitated the coming of the Son of God, born of a woman and dying a substitutionary death on man's behalf.

The Koran on the other hand totally rejects Jesus as the Son of God, yet claiming Him to be a prophetic. It claims itself as a revelation of God which begun with Abraham and continued throughout the Old Testaments Prophets. Take a look at what the Christian scripture had to say about those who do not accept Jesus as the Son of God.

> "22 Who is a liar but he that denieth that Jesus is the Christ? He is antichrist that denieth the Father and the Son. Whosoever denieth the Son, the same hath not the Father: (but) he that acknowledgeth the Son hath the Father also." (1 John 2:22 & 23)

Either Jesus is the Son of God, or he is the greatest liar that has ever lived. On numerous occasions Jesus Himself claimed He was God, and for the Koran to say He is a good prophet, is an indictment of Jesus or the Koran. If Jesus was just a good prophet, He would have perpetuated one of the greatest lies in the history of mankind, and how could such a liar be a prophet. Listen to the testimony of Jesus as recorded in the book of John:

> John 8:56 56 "Your father Abraham rejoiced to see my day: and he saw it, and was glad. 57 Then said the Jews unto him, Thou art not yet fifty years old, and hast thou seen Abraham? 58 Jesus said unto them, Verily, verily, I say unto you, Before Abraham was, I am. John 17:5 And now, O Father, glorify thou me with thine own self with the glory which I had with thee before the world was."

Furthermore, both Old Testament and New Testament scripture attest to the divinity of the Messiah who would and did come.

> "1 Corinthians 8:6 But to us there is but one God, the Father, of whom are all things, and we in him; and one Lord Jesus Christ, by whom are all things, and we by him."
>
> "Phil 2:5 5 Let this mind be in you, which was also in Christ Jesus: 6 Who, being in the form of God, thought it not robbery to be equal with God: 7 But made himself of no reputation, and took upon him the form of a servant, and was made in the likeness of men:"
>
> "Colossians 1:15 15 Who is the image of the invisible God, the firstborn of every creature: 16 For by him were all things created, that are in heaven, and that

# LORD OF ZION

*are in earth, visible and invisible, whether they be thrones, or dominions, or principalities, or powers: all things were created by him, and for him: 17 And he is before all things, and by him all things consist."*

*"Hebrew 1:8 8 But unto the Son he saith, Thy throne, O God, is for ever and ever: a scepter of righteousness is the scepter of thy kingdom. 9 Thou hast loved righteousness, and hated iniquity; therefore God, even thy God, hath anointed thee with the oil of gladness above thy fellows. 10 And, Thou, Lord, in the beginning hast laid the foundation of the earth; and the heavens are the works of thine hands: 11 They shall perish; but thou remainest; and they all shall wax old as doth a garment; 12 And as a vesture shalt thou fold them up, and they shall be changed: but thou art the same, and thy years shall not fail."*

Islam claims all revelations given to others before Mohammed are binding upon their people. It asserts God will judge them from their individual books, yet it is seeking to make proselytes of both Jews and Gentiles. Any believer of the Bible is forced to say the Koran is in direct opposition to the Bible, and contradicts it, how then can they both be Holy?

## BLACK MUSLIMS – NATION OF ISLAM

Black Muslims is a widely used name for the adherents of an American Black nationalist religious movement once called "The Lost-Found Nation of Islam" and "The World Community of Islam" and now "The Nation of Islam."

The movement began in 1930 when Wallace Fard began preaching a separatist message attracting 8,000 followers in four years before disappearing in June 1934. It is said that Fard was a white man, and it is interesting that a white man would begin preaching that white people are devils. This suggests that this movement was created by someone to sought to infiltrate and discredit the black community, although

**103**

the plan seems to have backfired, as the Nation, has grown and thrived in recent years.

The movement, now headquarters in Chicago, grew under Fard's successor Elijah Mohammed. Elijah saw himself as the "prophet and apostle of Allah," and called upon Black men to fight the white Devils. Elijah is best known for His feud with Malcolm X which resulted in Malcolm death.

Malcolm X grew up with parents who were followers of Marcus Garvey, and regular attendee's of the Seventh Day Adventist Church. He was converted to Islam in 1947 while imprisoned, but later broke with the movement. This happened because he was being taught the white man was the devil, and when he took his pilgrimage to Mecca he discovered many of Islam's followers were indeed white. Furthermore, he was aware of the sexual exploits of Elijah Mohammed, and was not willing to be a puppet anymore.

The movement was later dissolved by Mohammed Son, who was trying to bring it back to the Muslims teaching, but a splinter group led by Louis Farrakhan, retains the earlier separatist principles and the name "Nation of Islam."

The Muslims has monopolized the conversion of Black men. Their strategy is to win Black men in America, because therein lies the future of the Black race, a noble goal.

Unfortunately history has taught us that wherever Islam takes a stronghold, has meant the demise of that nation. Women are treated as inferior, education is lacking and living standard is poor even thought Muslim leaders are among some of the wealthiest people in the world.

It is true that many people of African descent are thirsting for someone to tell them what the future holds and hungry to find a place of belonging and meaning for there existence in an environment hazardous to their health. Many are finding solace in the Muslim movement, because it makes them feel

## LORD OF ZION

good about themselves, and empowers them - something the Christian church has neglected to do through the years.

Does this mean however that we should sit back and watch the black male being grasped by the claws of Islam? Do we have a responsibility to show that there are good reasons for members of the Black Race to accept Jesus as Lord of their lives? Can we help Africans everywhere to understand that what is needed is not just a fulfilling life on earth, but also an eternal existence as citizens of Zion. These are the questions the black church must ask itself, and these answers can only be found in the context I believe of the Christian movement.

## JESUS CHRIST BCE 4 - CE 27

Jesus Christ was born in Bethlehem Judea around BCE 4 in a world impact by Greek culture, and dominated by the Romans. Judea had been ruled by the Persians from the end of the Babylonian captivity in 536, then Alexander the Great, the Ptolemy's of Egypt, the Seleucids of Syria and then the Maccabees, who were local Jewish leaders. The Romans took over from About BCE (Before the Christian Era) 63 and continued their rule under Herod and His family until the nation ceased to exist in AD 70 with the destruction of Jerusalem.[54]

Herod murdered many members of the Maccabees family when the Romans placed him in charged and this caused him to be hated. This hatred grew even greater because of his oppressive taxes. It was one of these taxes that forced a woman name Mary and her husband Joseph to travel to Bethlehem where their child Jesus was born.

Mary and Joseph were the parents of Jesus and they had received a vision from God telling them they were to be the parents of the Son of God. This was especially important to Joseph, because when he discovered Mary was pregnant and

---

[54]Horn, Siegfried H., *Seventh-day Adventist Bible Dictionary*,
(Washington, D.C.: Review and Herald Publishing Association) 1979.

he was not the father, he was going to put her away. The angel informed him however that this child was God's son and that he would be the Savior of the world.

Herod's last act just before he died in BCE 4 was to kill all the male infants (Matthew 2) in a bid to destroy Jesus, who Herod learned about from the wise men who had traveled from their distant lands of Egypt, Ethiopia and Arabia to see the messiah.[55]

According to the Bible, Jesus was born in a stable, grew up in the poor community of Nazareth and began his ministry at age 27 and worked for only three and a half years before he was killed by the Romans on a cross at Calvary.

The name Jesus was very common among the Jews and expressed their faith in God's promise to bring salvation through his Son. Mary and Joseph however name their son Jesus because the Angel Gabriel appeared to them prior to his birth and informed them that this should be the child's name because he would save His people from their sins.(Matthew 1:21)

The name Christ on the other hand was not a personal name, but a Title used to identify him Jesus as the Messiah. The early Christians saw Christ:

> *"As the One in whom the Messianic promises and prophecies of the OT met their fulfillment. To those who believed in Him as sent of God He was the Christ, that is, the Messiah, the One "anointed" by God to be the Savior of the world. When used together, as in Mt 1:18; 16:20; Mk 1:1, the 2 names Jesus and Christ constitute a confession of faith that Jesus of Nazareth, the Son of*

---

[55]Horn, Siegfried H., *Seventh-day Adventist Bible Dictionary*, (Washington, D.C.: Review and Herald Publishing Association) 1979.

# LORD OF ZION

> *Mary, is indeed the Christ, the Messiah (Mt 1:1; Acts 2:38).*[56]

In three and a half years of ministry, Jesus, cleansed lepers, raised the dead, turned water into wine, controlled nature, fed thousands with five loaves and two fishes, forgave sins, paid his taxes from money taken from a fishes mouth, open the eyes of the blind, unstopped the years of the deaf and even walked on water. For all his troubles, he was hounded constantly by the Jewish authorities, falsely accused, crucified on a cross and was laid to rest in a borrowed tomb, before he resurrected Himself and went to heaven one Sunday morning. Many modern Christians now use the resurrection as the reason to celebrate the first day Sabbath in opposition to the Seventh Day Sabbath Jesus and his disciples observed and the Bible commands.

## PROOF OF JESUS' LORDSHIP.

> *LUKE 24:25 "Then he said unto them, O fools, and slow of heart to believe all that the prophets have spoken: LUKE 24:26 Ought not Christ to have suffered these things, and to enter into his glory? LUKE 24:27 And beginning at Moses and all the prophets, he expounded unto them in all the scriptures the things concerning himself."*

This experience taken from the New Testament scripture gives the bases upon which Blacks today can accept Jesus. It was a few days after His resurrection when Jesus, unknowingly to his disciples, accompanied them as they traveled on the road to Emmaus. As they walked together, they talked about the happenings of the past few days, and sighed at their hope that Jesus was the one who was to redeem Israel. Christ them chided them for not knowing the scriptures. He informed them

---

[56]Horn, Siegfried H., *Seventh-day Adventist Bible Dictionary*, (Washington, D.C.: Review and Herald Publishing Association) 1979.

things went exactly as God through His prophets said it would. Then, beginning at Moses and the prophets, He revealed to them the things concerning Himself.

Just three days before He had been crucified, yet Christ did not want to establish their faith on something they had seen, but upon the testimony of the word of God.  Instead of showing them the nail marks in His hands and feet, instead of showing the wounds in His side, and His scarred mark forehead, He reviewed the prophetic forecasts of the coming of the Messiah, and revealed the predictions of the Old Testament prophets.

Thus their faith was established not upon the evidence of their senses but upon the certainty of God's word.  With confidence they went out to proclaim the Christ of prophecy.  They declared that hundreds of years before Jesus was born, the prophets told of His coming.  Thus they claimed Christ was the fulfillment of prophecy, the very embodiment of the Godhead, the Son of God made flesh.  This indeed was the testimony of Philip.

> *JOHN 1:45 "Philip findeth Nathanael, and saith unto him, We have found him, of whom Moses in the law, and the prophets, did write, Jesus of Nazareth, the son of Joseph."*

Speaking of the mighty preacher of Ephesus, an African born in Alexandria Doctor Luke writes:

> *Acts 18:28" For he mightily convinced the Jews, and that publicly, shewing by the scriptures that Jesus was Christ."*

Jesus Himself proved His claim to divinity on the basis of His fulfillment of Old Testament Prophecy.

## HIS BIRTH

# LORD OF ZION

> *Micah 5:2 "But thou, Bethlehem Ephratah, though thou be little among the thousands of Judah, yet out of thee shall he come forth unto me that is to be ruler in Israel; whose goings forth have been from of old, from everlasting."*

Out of the thousands of places the Messiah could be born, the Prophet Micah points out the exact location. The holy family lived in Nazareth, and had no intention of moving to Bethlehem. Just a week before Jesus was born, a decree came that all men should return home to be taxed. This forced Christ's parents to move to God's designated spot for the birth of their Son. Thus Christ the child of Prophecy was born in the town of Bethlehem. Let us note some of the other prophecies which prove beyond a shadow of a doubt the Divinity of Jesus.

> *ISAIAH 7:14 "Therefore the Lord himself shall give you a sign; Behold, a virgin shall conceive, and bear a son, and shall call his name Immanuel. GENESIS 49:10 The scepter shall not depart from Judah, nor a lawgiver from between his feet, until Shiloh come; and unto him shall the gathering of the People be."*

## BETRAYED BY FRIENDS

> *PSALM 55:12 "For it was not an enemy that reproached me; then I could have borne it: neither was it he that hated me that did magnify himself against me; then I would have hid myself from him" 13 But it was thou, a man mine equal, my guide, and mine acquaintance. 14 We took sweet counsel together, and walked unto the house of God in company."*

## PRICE OF BETRAYAL

ZECHARIAH 11:12 *"And I said unto them, If ye think good, give me my price; and if not, forbear. So they weighed for my price thirty pieces of silver."*

## NO BROKEN BONES:

*Psalm 34:20 "He keepeth all his bones: not one of them is broken."*

## RESURRECTION:

*Mat 28:1 " In the end of the Sabbath, as it began to dawn toward the first day of the week, came Mary Magdalene and the other Mary to see the sepulcher. Mat 28:2 And, behold, there was a great earthquake: for the angel of the Lord descended from heaven, and came and rolled back the stone from the door, and sat upon it. Mat 28:3 His countenance was like lightning, and his raiment white as snow: Mat 28:4 And for fear of him the keepers did shake, and became as dead men. Mat 28:5 And the angel answered and said unto the women, Fear not ye: for I know that ye seek Jesus, which was crucified. Mat 28:6 He is not here: for he is risen, as he said. Come, see the place where the Lord lay. Mat 28:7 And go quickly, and tell his disciples that he is risen from the dead; and, behold, he goeth before you into Galilee; there shall ye see him: lo, I have told you.*

*Mat 28:8 And they departed quickly from the sepulchre with fear and great joy; and did run to bring his disciples word. Mat 28:9 And as they went to tell his disciples, behold, Jesus met them, saying, All hail. And they came and held him by the feet, and worshipped."*

Jesus is now in heaven sitting at the right hand of the Father. He demonstrated his ability to raise us from the dead, by raising Himself. He has promised that one day he will return to

## LORD OF ZION

earth to rescue us and take us to Zion, a city which will be built by God Himself. Indeed to trust any other than Jesus would be to put our citizenship in jeopardy. Won't you accept Jesus today, so you too can be numbered among, the citizens of Zion?

# INDEX OF BIBLE REFERENCES USED

"Psalm 34:20, 109
1 Corinthians 8:6, 102
2 Corinthians 5:17, 61
2 King 19:34, 14
2 Samuel 11:, 86
2 SAMUEL 12:24, 86
2 Samuel 2:6, 13
Acts 18:28, 108
Acts 2:38, 106
Amos 9:7, 80
Colossians 1:15 15, 102
DAN 4:34, 61
DAN 4:5, 56
Dan 7:25, 31
Dan 7:7, 30
Daniel 4:10-17, 57
Daniel 4:24-27, 58
Daniel 4:30, 60
Daniel 7:23-25, 25
Exodus 20:4, 29
Ezekiel 28:2-5, 71
Ezra 9:2, 14, 86
*Genesis 10*, 13, 15, 89
GENESIS 10:1, 51
Genesis 10:6 & 15, 65
Genesis 10:6, 13 & 14, 79
Genesis 2:1-3, 24
Genesis 20:4), 82
Genesis 20:6, 83
GENESIS 41:50, 42
GENESIS 49:10, 109
Hebrew 1:8, 103
HEBREWS 11:16, 21
Hebrews 5:10, 12

Hebrews 7
Hebrews 7:, 16
Isaiah 11:11, 97
Isaiah 41:10, 48
ISAIAH 43:3, 96
Isaiah 66:22, 23
ISAIAH 7:14, 109
Isaiah 8:20, 101
Jeremiah 3:17, 14
JOHN 1:45, 108
John 17:5, 102
John 8:56 56, 102
Joshua 1:3-6, 48
Joshua 2:1 & 17, 85
Judges 1 and 3, 18
Judges 1:21, 18
Judges 1:27-33, 86
Judges 3:, 19
Judges 3:5, 14
LUKE 24:25, 107
Luke 4:8, 28
MAT 1:5, 86
MAT 23:37, 16
Mat 28:1, 110
Micah 5:2, 108
Mt 1:1, 106
Phil 2:5, 102
Psalm 105:23, 40
Psalm 105:27, 40
Psalm 106:22, 40
PSALM 55:12, 109
Psalm 78:51, 39
Psalm 87, 11
Psalm 87:2, 12

LORD OF ZION

Psalm 87:3, 21
Psalm 87:4, 37
Psalm 87:6, 99
Psalms 48:2, 14
Psalms 76:2, 14
Revelation 14:7, 31
Revelation 21, 22
Revelation 21:1, 21

Revelation 22:18-19, 100
ZECHARIAH 11:12, 109
Zechariah 8:, 17
Zechariah 8:1, 17
Zechariah 9:3-6, 77
Zechariah 9:3-6), 83
Zechariah 9:6-9, 84

# Bibliography

Arrian. The Campaigns of Alexander. London: Penguin Books. October 1976.

Bruce, F. F. The New Testament Documents. 5th rev. ed. Grand Rapids: Eerdmans, 1970.

Bruce, F. F. Tradition: Old and New, The Formation of the Christian Bible. Trans. J. A. Baker. Philadelphia: Fortress, 1972.

Carroll, Harry J., ed. The development of Civilization; a documentary history of politics, society and thoughts. Glenview, Ill. Scott, Foresman 1969.

CompuServe, Grolier Electronic Encyclopedia. Jewelry.

Diop, Cheikh Anta. Civilization or Barbarism. NY: Lawrence Hill Books. 1991 Edition: 1st edition.

Earl, R. How We Got Our Bible. Kansas City: Beacon Hill, 1971.

Ewert, David. From Ancient Tablets to Modern Translations. Grand Rapids: Zonderman Publishing House, 1922.

Finegan, J. Encountering New Testament Manuscripts. Grand Rapids: Eerdmans, 1974.

General Conference of 7th Day Adventist. Our firm foundation: A report of the Seventh Day Adventist Bible Conference held September 1-13. 1952. Washington DC: Review and Herald Publishing Association, 1953.

Horn, Siegfried H., Seventh-day Adventist Bible Dictionary Washington, D.C.: Review and Herald Publishing Association 1979.

Houston, Drusilla. Wonderful Ethiopians of the ancient Cushite Empire. Oklahoma City, Oklahoma: The Universal publishing co. 1926.

Hunt, G. About the New English Bible. Oxford and Cambridge University Press, 1927.

Hyman, M. Blacks who died for Jesus. Philadelphia: Corrective Black History Books. 1983.

Irvin L. Jenson, Journey of the Bible, the remarkable story of how the Bible came from God to you. Minneapolis, Minn.: World Wide Publications, c1990.

Josephus, Flavious. The Antiquities of the Jews. London: Printed for J. Cooke, No. 17, Pater-noster-Row, [1785-1786]

Keisler, N. L. and Nix, W. E. From God to us. Chicago: Moody, 1974.

Kenyon, F. G. Our Bible and the Ancient Manuscripts. Revised by A. W. Adams. New York: Harper and Brothers 1958.

Library of the Future, CDROM, History of Herodotus. Series 2nd ed., version 4.01.Garden Grove, CA: World Library, c1992.

Madhubuti, R. Haki, Black Men Obsolete, Single and Dangerous. NY, 1990, Third World Press

McKissi, Dwight. Beyond Roots, The search for Blacks in the Bible. Wenonah, NJ: Renaissance Productions, 1974.

Pehausen, Hans von. The Formation of the Christian Bible. Translated J A. Baker. Philadelphia: Fortress, 1972.

Reumann, J. H. P. Four Centuries of the English Bible. Philadelphia: Muhlenberg, 1961.

Reumann, J. H. The Romance of Bible Scripts and Scholars Englewood Cliffs: Prentice-Hill, 1965.

Shinnie, Margaret. Ancient African Kingdoms. New York St. Martins Press, 1965.

White, E. G. Spirit if Prophecy Vol. 1. Mountain View California: Pacific Press Publishing Association.

White, E. G. The Signs of the Times, February 1880.

Williams, Chancellor. The Destruction of Black Civilization Chicago Illinois: Third World Press, 1976.

Williams, Richard: They stole it, But You Must Return it. Rochester NY, 1986, HEMA Publishing, 1986.